LITTLE PEOPLE OF ASIA

LITTLE PEOPLE OF ASIA

By

OLIVE THORNE MILLER

GYAN

Published by

Gyan Publishing House
5, Ansari Road
Daryaganj, New Delhi-110002
Phone: 011-47034999, 9811692060
E-mail: books@gyanbooks.com

Distribution Network
gyanbooks.com
India, USA, Canada, UK, Australia, France

ISBN : 978-81-212-6336-8 (PB)
First Published, 1883

2nd Impression 2022

Printed at: Gyan Press, Delhi.

LITTLE PEOPLE OF ASIA
Author: Olive Thorne Miller

IN SCHOOL. *Frontispiece, Page 376*

LITTLE PEOPLE OF ASIA

BY

OLIVE THORNE MILLER

GOING TO SCHOOL.—PAGE 314.

1883

CONTENTS.

Little People of Asia.

CHAPTER I.

TO BEGIN.

THERE are many queer things in this big world of ours, but there's nothing queerer, I think, than the way children live in different parts of it.

I have always wondered how the little Turks pass away their time, what they play with, and how they feel, bundled up like rolls of dry-goods. I have great curiosity to know how it would feel to be a China girl or boy, and have feet three inches long, or the hair all shaved off the head; and I've tried to fancy how it would seem to live in a tent like a Tartar youngster, never knowing this week where one will be the next, and thinking a horse is the finest thing in the world.

Well; being so interested in the ways of little people, I have been for many years trying to find out about them. I said to myself, "I will learn what the youngsters do all over the world; what they play, what they have to eat, what sort of clothes they wear, and then I will put it all in a beautiful book for our own little people to read;" and thinking so, I went to work.

IN A BASKET.

But, dear me! what a time I had! What shelves full of books I waded through, turning over page after page and chapter after chapter of travels, about bad roads, and untidy hotels where one couldn't get anything fit to eat, and about the weather, and the small discomforts of travelers—just to find now and then a chance word about the children.

I almost began to think there were no children in those far-off countries, for you know—or if you do not I will tell you—that most grown-up travelers fill their books with talk about the big folks, and the sights of the country, and sprinkle them pretty thickly with their own troubles in getting about, and for any notice they take of little people they might as well be blind.

Studies by the way-side

But I would not be discouraged. I had set my heart on telling you young people all about your little playfellows on the other side of the globe, so I kept on digging in the big books, and I looked over all the papers and magazines, and I went to see everybody I could hear of who had been in those far-off countries, and I asked—O! as many questions as any of you curious boys or girls could do yourself—and all for the book I wanted to make for you.

And now here it is, and I hope you'll like it. I have gathered here a bit and there a bit, and have tried to be very sure that every word is true.

The curious things that I've found out about little folks begin at the very beginning; for nothing is more strange than the way people treat babies. Having his head shaved clean as the back of his hand, is not specially queer to a youngster who had a boiling hot omelet poultice on the same head before he was two days old—is it now?

IN ARMS

Three inch long feet are not odd to an unfortunate girl who had her wrists tied together when a baby to make her truthful; dressing in stripes of paint, with loads of brass jewelry, can't be much of a surprise to one who spent every day of baby life half buried in the ground, set out like a plant.

Living in a six-foot tent, and never having any bigger house, comes natural enough to a child whose only cradle was a shoe.

You think I'm joking? Far from it! These are not half the wonders that happen every day in the world. Let me tell you.

It is the mother of Guinea who buries her baby alive, up to its waist, in warm sand; and it is to keep it out of mischief while she works. The little Lapp is the youngster whose cradle is a shoe—a big affair, covered with skin and stuffed with soft moss, in which he can either be hung to a tree, or covered up in the snow while Mamma goes to church.

The Eskimo carries her baby inside her fur sack, at the back of her neck, and our own Indians strap baby to a board, and sling him over the shoulders.

QUEER BABY CARRIAGE.

In India the babies ride in a basket hanging from Mamma's head, as you see on page 10, or on her hip, or in a hammock, as in the little way-side sketch, or, in some parts they are adorned with a nose-ring, like their mother's, and wrapped up in a veil like her also.

In China they're tied to an older child's back, and among the Mongolians they travel about in bags slung on a camel's side.

IN A BAG

One mother lays her baby where a stream of water will fall on its head, to make it tough, she says; another covers hers with paste, and a third hangs hers in baskets from a straight sup-

IN A HAMMOCK.

port, as you see in the picture on page 12, where the family have stopped to rest, and left the little ones in their baskets ready to be carried on their journey again.

The Bulgarian mother it is who puts a hot omelet to the little one's head, to make it solid and protect it from sunstroke; and the Bulgarian baby doesn't like it any better than you would. He makes a great row about it, I assure you.

The Turkoman Mamma carries her little one in a hammock, as you see on the preceding page; but the queerest cradle of all is this from Central Asia.

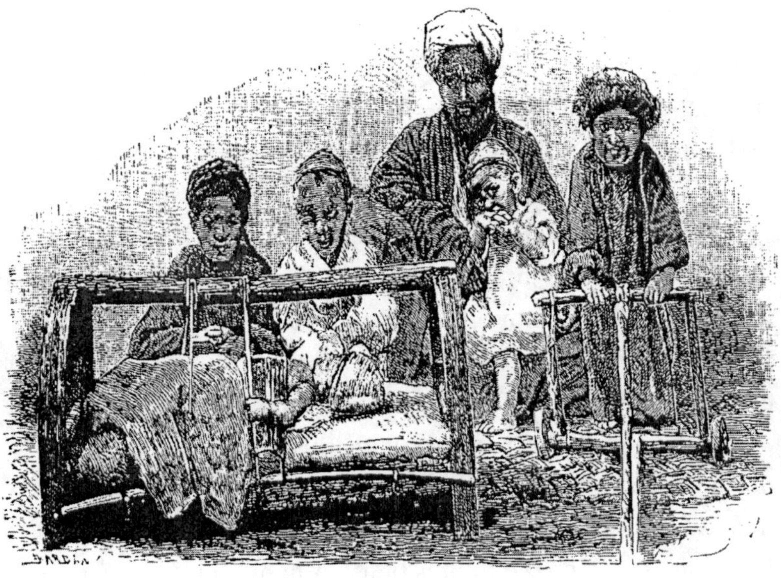

THE ODDEST CRADLE OF ALL.

CHAPTER II.

THE SALTED BABY; THE LITTLE TURK.

THE Turkish Mamma salts her precious baby. Perhaps this is the queerest of all, and it is for the same reason that we salt meat—to keep it sweet!

This is one of the least of the odd things that happen to him. After his salting comes dressing, such as it is, and it is only a little shirt! Oh, yes! and a red silk cap on the head, with a pearl tassel, and some gold coins and charms to keep away evil.

But after dressing comes wrapping up, for the poor little Turk baby is made into a bundle, so that he can stir neither hand nor foot, and only move his head. This is the way they do it: A quilt is prepared, a yard square; this is laid out on the floor and one corner turned down. On the quilt, baby in his shirt and cap is laid cornerwise, with his head over the turned-down corner. Then the corners of the quilt are brought up over him, after his toes are carefully turned in, and his arms laid flat to his sides. Over the quilt is tightly wound a long strip of cloth, and the baby is a perfect mummy.

That is dreadful enough, but worse is to come. First he gets his name in this gentle way: His father takes him in his arms, carries him *behind the door* (!) mutters a prayer over him, and then shouts in his poor little ear, three times, the name which has been selected for him. I suppose he thinks baby is deaf!

Then comes the cradle, and I wish you could see the torture-box called by that name (or *beshik*, which means cradle). It is a long, narrow box on two rockers. The ends of the rockers come up over the top and have a rail across, on which the nurse leans to feed the baby; for when once he gets in he has to stay, I can tell you. No use to cry to come up; "coming up" is almost unknown to him.

In the box is a hard mattress, and no pillow, and in this, on his back, the poor little baby bundle is laid. Lest he should prove refractory and get out—with all that wrapping up—they tie him in!

On his breast and his knees are laid small cushions, so that the binding will not press on him; a red gauze veil is thrown over him, and thus he is left half a day at a time. When he is hungry he is, perhaps, fed, and the rest of the time he amuses himself with a little sugar and bread tied up in a rag.

Poor baby! If after all this he is restless, he gets a dose of opium or something similar, and then he is quiet enough. Some babies lie all the time in a stupid, dozing state; all of them are injured by it, and many of them go from their cruel cradles to their little graves.

If anything ails a child, it is thought to be the "evil eye," and some old woman is called in to breathe on it. If that fails, they call in the most celebrated sheikh they can find, and *he* breathes on it, and puts on a charm (made of garlic, alum, and a verse of the Koran, all sewed up in little triangles of blue cloth), and a few amulets of blue glass, such as horseshoes, little hands, and so forth.

If all these wonderful things fail to cure the child, and he dies, the easy-going parents wipe their tears, say it is *kismet*, and go on with their usual duties. By *kismet* they mean what we call fate. "Whatever is to be, will be," they say, and there's no use mourning about it.

Perhaps there are no more superstitious people on the round globe than these same Turks. Nothing happens to them without supernatural agency, as they believe. If anything is lost, some one cast the "evil eye" on it; if you look sharply at one, you are casting the "evil eye" on him. Every action has regard to omens; nothing can be done unless the signs are right. They believe in dreams, they believe in magic, they believe in "spells;" there's nothing supernatural that they do not believe in.

We may laugh at this, but it is a serious matter to them, a matter of life and death. Many a girl has died because she thought herself bewitched.

I haven't told you all the things that happen to the baby Turk. When he is two days old invitations are sent out for his first reception, to take place on the next day. It is not done by means of cards, nor of written notes; instead, each person invited receives a bottle of sherbet, a drink made of candied sugar and spices.

The third day the house is thrown open to visitors, and everybody comes who chooses, whether invited or not. If he is invited, however, he has dinner served to him; but if not, he has to content himself with sherbet.

This is an affair of great ceremony. Bands of music are on hand to escort the most important guests in, and each guest is preceded by a servant bearing a gift. If the family is well-to-do the present is a basket of sweets, prettily arranged with flowers and gilt paper, wrapped in gauze, and tied up with ribbons; but if poor, the gift takes a useful form, coffee or provisions.

Mamma, gorgeously but rather uncomfortably arrayed and placed, receives her lady guests, who say to her, "Wonderful! let it be long-lived and happy."

And now comes a queer thing. *We* should hasten to look at the baby, and say nice and pleasant things about it; but if we did, its mother would be very angry at us. The Turkish ladies scarcely look at it. If they speak of it at all, they call it "ugly," or "naughty," or "dirty;" and if one ventured so far as to look at the poor little creature, it is instantly *spat upon*—to protect it from harm.

Still worse; every guest is suspected of throwing an "evil eye" on the child, and the moment one goes, measures are taken to see if it has been done. How do you suppose thay find out? They throw cloves on the fire! This is not fun, it is dead earnest; and if a clove happens to burst in burning, there's a great hue and cry, and the most violent efforts made to avert the bad effects.

These efforts are worthy of the cause. A lock of hair from the baby and one from its mother are solemnly burnt; prayers are said, blows are given over the child, and he is spat upon till his friends think he is sufficiently treated.

Another thing: Baby must never be left alone for an instant, or he will become possessed by certain evil spirits. Not even his mother can protect him from this, but if he *must* be left, as in poor families he sometimes is, a broom standing beside him will guard him from danger.

On the eighth day comes the next great ceremony in the little Turk's life; he goes to the public bath. This is a great affair. Company is invited, and they march in procession, baby on the lead. Each family sends carpets and bathing linen, and there they all spend the day, having refreshments served, and going through various ceremonies considered necessary on the occasion. The worst, as usual, happens to the baby; he has hot water thrown over his poor little body, and he is rubbed and scrubbed till he shrieks and screams like any little westerner of you all.

After this there are for some time no more special ceremonies; baby lies in his mummy case, in his box-like cradle, sucks his sugar rag, sleeps his opium sleep, and is rocked from morning till night, and from night till morning. The rocking-string is never out of the hand of mother or nurse. No wonder the black-eyed Turkish baby grows solemn and quiet, looking at life with calm indifference, seldom laughing or crying, never kicking or crowing. He can't kick; he has nothing to laugh at; he doesn't know how to crow. It is not surprising that a Turk can sit on a carpet all day long, sipping coffee, smoking and talking, or listening to story-telling. It is no wonder that he is never in a hurry, that he regards time as something to be gotten rid of. If he can't do a thing to-day he may be able to do it to-morrow, and in any case he maintains a repose which we hurrying western people can never attain.

When the baby grows old enough to kick, in spite of his wrappings, he is allowed to creep about. Then, too, he begins to eat something besides milk; and how do you suppose the tender Turkish mother teaches her baby to eat?

She prepares a little basket of food, all kinds of fruits and sweet things, and gives it to the little one to help itself. The child eats whenever it feels like it, and whatever it fancies, from the basket. Hundreds of Turkish babies die every year from this one cause.

IN A TURKISH HOUSE.

These are queer ways, to be sure. Let me tell you what a queer house he lives in. In the first place, when you come up to it in the street, you see nothing but a high wall, with a mean-looking door in it. You'd think you were going into some warehouse or other unattractive place. But inside—if it was the house of a well-to-do man—you would find a delightful yard or court, with fountains and trees and flowers, and built around this yard on all four sides you would see the house.

A fine Turkish house is a beautiful thing to see. Our little salted baby—if his papa has plenty of money—has grand rooms to live in, such as you have read about in the Arabian Nights, and even more beautiful, some people say.

Here is a picture of part of an elegant Turkish room to show you how they look, and how the walls are made. The windows you see, are very large and open almost the whole wall. On the farther side you see the divan, the only seat in a Turkish house. It is a wide, low lounge, running around three sides of the room generally, and covered with some gay-colored stuff, with big pillows leaning against the wall. On this the people sit, with feet drawn up under them.

Not a table or a chair; not a book, paper, or magazine; not a picture nor a nick-nack in sight; not one of the dozens of things we think we must have. What sort of people live here?

Look at them. Here's the mother in her own room, the harem. She half sits up among her pillows on the divan. She has very full trousers, which fall in folds over her ankles, as you can see in the young girl who is standing up, taking a scolding from the old servant on the floor. Then she has a gold-embroidered jacket of velvet or satin, and perhaps a cashmere shawl around her waist.

IN A TURKISH HAREM.

Her long hair—which you cannot see in the picture—is braided in ever so many fine braids, with gold pieces and jewelry hanging all over them; and when she is dressed she has loads of jewels on arms, and hands, and neck, and head, and ears, and ankles, and even toes; everywhere she can hang a precious stone or a gold ornament she hangs one, and a gorgeous object she is to behold.

And that isn't all. Around her head and shoulders is a veil, her feet are bare, and she is smoking a pipe, or more politely a *narghilé*. You see it standing on the floor, under the care of the old servant, while the lady holds the mouth-piece in her hand.

A strange looking mother, to be sure! But how does the father look? Here he is in his own part of the house—for Turkish houses, however poor, are always in two parts, the women's, or the harem, and the men's, and they are as separate as though they were under different roofs.

His room is as big and as bare as hers, and there he sits cross-legged among his cushions, with wide trowsers that hang like a skirt when he walks, a wadded dressing-gown, generally held together by a rich shawl, and on his head a turban. If he isn't smoking he is drinking coffee.

There you have the father and mother; they're not much like yours, you see, at least on the outside.

How about the children? Well; they look about as odd, to our eyes. The boy dresses exactly like his grave papa, in turban and wide trowsers, pointed slippers, and a dressing gown, and the girl is a copy of mamma, in silks and satins, with embroidery and jewels, and pink dye on fingers and toes, and a veil, if she's old enough.

But you don't see how people live in such a house! How do

A TURKISH PAPA.

they eat without a table to hold the dinner? how do they keep warm without a fire? how do they light the house without gas, or a place to stand a lamp?

I'll tell you how the little Turks pass their day. When they hear that their father is up, and taking his coffee—which is all he takes for breakfast, they jump out of bed and run and ask him for money.

In their night-clothes? I hear you cry.

Alas, children! Turks have no night-clothes; they sleep in their day garments. In the same wadded dressing-gown sort of a coat that he wears always in the house, the boy lies down to sleep; and in all her in-door finery of silks and satins, the girl does the same. So do their father and mother, and so does nearly everybody. No fuss of dressing, you see. I'm afraid you boys would like that. A new garment is put on once for all, and worn night and day till worn out, or given away.

Don't forget, by the way, that I am telling you about Turkish customs, as they have been for ages, and not about the ways of Turks who have been trying to live like Europeans, of late.

To go on with the children's day. They ask for money every morning; every Turkish youngster, down to the very beggars—and they generally get a little.

As soon as they leave their beds the slaves begin to roll them up from the floor.

From the floor! no bedsteads? Not a bedstead in all Turkey. At night, the slaves—which are the only servants among the Turks—spread on the floor for each one a mattress, or rather a bag of wool, then a sheet and narrow pillow, with linen case open at both ends, then a thick coverlid of satin or brocade (or chintz, if the people are poor), with the upper sheet sewed on to it.

In the morning the beds are rolled up and packed away in closets, and the room is ready for any use. So you see there's not only no bedstead, but no bedroom in the "Jewel," which the Turks consider their country.

A TURK AT HIS PRAYERS.

As soon as papa has finished his two or three cups of coffee, cups about the size of a big thimble, he prepares to go out. He lays off his dressing gown, puts on a long-sleeved vest and a coat or jacket of some sort, and goes to the bazar, if he's a merchant, or to the barber's, or a coffee-house, where he will sit and sip coffee, and smoke, and talk, or listen to story-telling all day, if he has no pressing business to attend to. But whatever he does you may be sure he never forgets to go through his prayers at certain appointed hours of every day.

When the hour arrives, the good Mohammedan spreads his prayer carpet on the floor, wherever he may be, turns his face toward the city of Mecca, and goes through certain forms. The pictures show two of the attitudes.

And mamma? Well, she plans her day; makes up her mind whether she will visit some friends or go and ride in her carriage

ANOTHER POSITION OF PRAYER.

(if she has one), or make a trip to the bazar to buy something, or whether she will go to the bath.

Meanwhile the children have been out, and spent their money on cakes and sweet things, and had something to eat, though the first regular meal is at ten or eleven o'clock. If they go to school they start off with their particular slave to take care of them, and an expensive school-bag to hold the Koran, their only school book. School is a droll place; no arithmetic and geography, no writing and drawing, nothing is taught but religion, the Koran, how to read it in Arabic, and sometimes what it means.

That is, usually. In some schools in Damascus writing is taught as well as arithmetic.

In these schools the boys sit on the floor, cross-legged, holding the paper in the left hands, and taking ink out of long brass inkstands worn in the girdles.

Where they learn only the Koran they are placed in rows, standing on their knees, and each one holding his book, from which he reads the lesson aloud, while he sways his body back and forth all the time;—one or two hundred together sometimes.

Different from your school, isn't it?

At one end of the room sits the master, on a mat, with pipe in one hand and rod in the other. Naughty boys are whipped with the rod, or decorated with a wooden hobble over the ankle.

You may laugh at this sort of a school, but it's a very important thing in the life of a little Turk. Nothing is done without certain ceremonies, and the first day in school is rather funny, —as we look at it.

To begin with, the child, who is always quite young when he enters school, has a new suit of clothes, and an expensive school-bag, with the Koran, as I told you.

Thus prepared his father leads him to school, and as a sort of examination before the teacher, he recites the creed, that is, you know, what all good Mohammedans believe.

This ceremony over, the new scholar kisses the teacher's hand, and then joins the class, and the father goes home.

This isn't all. After prayers are recited, the scholars form a procession, headed by the teacher, and lead home the new boy. As they go through the streets the teacher chants prayers, and the scholars respond to each one, "Amin! Amin!"

When they reach the boy's house the father meets them, offers refreshments, and what they probably like better, a piece of money (about one cent), to each schoolmate of his son. Then comes a rush into the street to find some peddler of sweets, and in a few minutes every cent is spent.

This curious ceremony is repeated at the first examination, when the teacher is presented with some money and clothes.

Out of school hours the youngsters do their best to have a good time. The poor children play in the streets, make mud pies, and paddle in the water, as they do nearer home; while the boys and girls of richer houses play around the house or the court.

I told you about the court, you remember. It is a delightful place generally, and entirely hidden from the world outside. Here the children play, and here the father comes to spend the cool hours of a summer evening.

But what do the children have for playthings? Now, alas! I know you will feel sorry for your poor little Turk, when I give you a list of the playthings, for I can give you a list. Think of a list of your playthings! Think of the hundreds of different things in a toy-shop and then hear what these children have.

The girls have a miserable apology for a doll—it is impossible to imagine a girl who never had a doll—made of bundles of rags, and a cradle for the same. The boys have rattles and trumpets, and at certain seasons of the year a figure, a sort of punchinello, made of wood and daubed with bright-colored paint, without regard to where it should be put on.

They have also a few tops of terra cotta. That is all. No books or papers for them; a few games, such as "knuckle bones" (or jack-stones, as you say), ball, and bows and arrows; scarcely any other toys.

Even these are in spite of the teaching of Mohamet, their great prophet. He says this hard thing about the children: "Our religion forbids children to have any toys. Studies must be directed toward religion and war, and for that reason they must ride, and use the bow and gun, but nothing else."

Boys are meant to be grave little copies of their dignified papa, and they are funny little old men, when in their father's room, in the presence of guests. At such times the smallest Turk will walk in with the utmost dignity, make a low bow, and sit down gravely in the farther corner, speaking only when spoken to, and in every way trying to behave like a grown-up man.

This would be all very well if it would last, but, sad to say, no sooner does the boy get into the other part of the house than he acts like a very different person. He uses bad language, plays ill-natured jokes on the slaves, teases everybody, and if he cannot have what he wants, he stamps, and pounds, and screams, and behaves very badly indeed.

To return to their amusements. They partake of their mother's entertainments, for you must remember that Turkish women, kept secluded in the harem, with little education, are not much more than children themselves. Their principal enjoyments are shopping, visiting, and going to the bath. Whichever mamma decides to do she begins to prepare for the first thing in the morning.

She does not simply slip on a street dress and pair of walking boots, as does your mamma; she spends hours at her toilet. She first whitens her face to a fashionable shade with some cosmetic, and then rouges her cheeks. She blackens her eyebrows and eye-lashes; and after all that there are fifty things to be done before she is ready to put on her street garments; for, however much time she may spend on her dress, when she goes into the street she must look like every other Turkish lady, so that her dearest friend would not know her.

She puts on then a great wrap, a sort of cloak, which covers her all up, and a thick veil, which only allows her eyes to be seen. Now she looks like a bundle of dry goods, and now it is proper for her to go out.

Here is a picture of her in her street-dress, only when she goes out she will draw her cloak closely around her, and her veil tightly over her face.

If she has a carriage, the children will tease all the morning to go too; and after she has taken her seat, they run and scramble and quarrel to get seats also.

If a picnic is proposed, which it very often is, they drive out to some suitable place and spend the day, or what is left of it, sitting on carpets they have brought with them, eating sweets, smoking cigarettes, and chatting with their friends.

It is only when on a journey or some serious business that the Turk takes his wife out with him, as you see in the picture over the leaf, of the curious round boat called the *kufa*.

It reminds one of the three wise men of Gotham, who went to sea in a tub. But this boat is of basket-work, made water-tight, and it goes along fast enough for a Turk, who's never in a hurry, you know.

If a visit is what they go out for, they try to get to the

friend's house about sunrise, as that is the fashionable hour for a call. When they enter the house a curious greeting takes

GOING OUT.

place, as you see in the picture on page 35, of a formal call. Each lady touches her finger-tips to her heart, to her lips, and to her forehead; they then kiss each other on both cheeks, take off their veils and wraps and sit down.

Very soon coffee and sweets of some sort are brought in, and then cigarettes or pipes.

Queer as it seems to us, pipes are so commonly smoked by everybody that families have to keep a great many to offer to

A TURKISH BOAT.

guests, as well as some for the servants to use and offer to their friends.

In the same picture you see a Turkish child, and doesn't he look like his papa, cut down?

You would laugh to see refreshments served, that is, unless you were very well bred indeed. A servant comes to you with

A FORMAL CALL.

a tray, on which are two dishes of a sort of preserve or jam, cups of water, and two spoon-holders, one full of clean teaspoons, the other empty.

What would you do? If you were acquainted with Turkish manners you would do thus: take a clean teaspoon, dip it into one of the dishes of jam, put it in your mouth, follow it at once with a sip of water, as though it held a pill you must swallow, and then put the spoon into the empty glass.

The servant would pass on to the next guest, and the performance would be repeated. No one takes more than one taste, and everyone, of course, takes a clean spoon.

I spoke of the bath as an amusement. You do not see any fun in it, I presume, unless it's a bath in the sea on a fine day; but to the little Turks it's a holiday. Every house in Turkey has a bath, to begin with, if it's nothing more than a big earthen jar buried up to its rim in the ground, which the poorest have.

The finest houses have suits of rooms given up to this purpose, and the Turkish bath—as you perhaps know—has rooms of different degrees of heat, and is not a simple plunge into water like ours, but is a series of scrubbings, and punching, and kneading, and steaming, and shampooing, and resting, which requires at least an hour, and may be stretched out by those who like it, to last all day.

Well, when a Turkish family, that is to say, mother and children, start for the public bath, which they do every three or four weeks (no matter how fine a bath they may have at home), the slaves go ahead with bundles of clothes, towels, and refreshments, and the family come prepared to stay all day.

They make a sort of general visit of it, chatting with friends, exchanging items of news, telling stories, eating, and so forth. So they spend the whole day.

If mamma decides to go to the bazar, either to buy something, to get a letter written by professional writers, or to procure a charm to cure a disease, or bring harm to an enemy, the children have fine times.

The bazar, you must know, takes the place of our various shops. There, under a roof, in small sort of niches, sit old Turks, cross-legged, pipe in hand, to sell their wares. There one can buy anything the city furnishes; there also one can have jewelry made from his own gold, and see the jeweler make it, sitting on the ground before his tiny brasier.

In the bazar the youngsters find plenty of use for their money; they can buy a drink of sour milk, for instance. You cry out at that—I can hear you—but the young Turk likes it.

Then, if he wants to eat, he can buy a sheet of bread, like a pancake, and a skewer of chunks of meat, nicely browned in the oven. Or he can stop the old Turk who goes by, calling out:

"O, bountiful one! Cool and refreshing! Purify thy blood!" and out of his skin bottle he can have a drink of—what do you guess?—liquorice water! That you'd like, *I* know.

But wherever the family spends the day, they must be sure to be home before the dinner hour, which is about sunset. At that time papa Turk comes home, and what he would do if he found nobody there, I can't imagine. If he was like the Turks in our story books, I suppose he'd cut off their heads; but as he is not, he would probably tell them they must stay at home the next day.

Then comes dinner; and that is so very different from ours,

IN THE HAREM.

that I'm sure you'll like to hear about it. In the first place, the father eats his alone, or with guests if he has any, in his part of the house, and the mother eats hers with her children, or guests, in her part. It is considered very improper for gentlemen and ladies to eat together, as we do.

The first thing on serving dinner, is to bring in the table—not a big extension dining table like ours, but a sort of low stool, a foot or so high, and about the same in width, as you see in this picture, where the ladies are entertained by a musical slave.

On this is placed a round tray of copper, or gold, if the family is wealthy, containing a piece of thin bread for each person, and the salt or other condiments, that may be needed. No knives, forks, or napkins!—not a plate, or a glass, nor a cup, and no sign of a chair to sit on. How would you manage to eat?

As fingers take the place of forks, of course they should be clean, so the first business is to wash them. A slave, or perhaps two, comes around to every one in the room with a curious arrangement for the purpose. There is a basin with a perforated cover, so that the water once used may be out of sight, and a queer-shaped pitcher.

He (or she) comes to the first one, who holds the hands over the basin while he pours water over them. The hands are then dried on a gold-embroidered towel, which hangs over his arm, and he passes to the next. This done, the family gather around the table, sitting cross-legged on the floor. As many as eight can sit at one of these tiny tables.

Now comes dinner. It is brought in on a large tray and put on the floor, and each dish in turn is placed on the tray from which they eat. If soup is first, every one has a spoon, and all dip into the same dish. Then that is taken away and another dish put on. Each one takes what he likes, with his fingers of course, and puts it into his mouth, and so on till all is eaten, or has been removed.

"Horrid!" "Disgusting!" I hear you say, and so it seems to tell of it, but *seen* it is quite different. Only three fingers are used in the operation, the thumb and first two fingers of the left hand. The meat is cut in small pieces, and cooked to rags almost, so there is no cutting necessary, and after it is over the hand-washing comes in again. Then they return to their cushions, and coffee in cups about big enough for a doll, is served, and last of all, cigarettes or pipes.

After dinner come different amusements; no games, no plays in which the family join, but some sort of entertainment furnished by people hired for the purpose. It may be a professional story-teller, for this is one of the best loved amusements in Turkey. From the grave, turbaned papa himself, down to the meanest slave in the kitchen, every one delights in a story. The story-teller is seated in the place of honor, provided with refreshment, and the family gather around on the floor, or on the divan, to listen, while tall candles, or lamps on tall standards, are set on the floor.

Shall I tell you one? Would you like to listen to a genuine Turkish story, which has no doubt been told a thousand times in coffee-houses, in harems, in barber shops, all over Turkey?

Well; I thought you would like one, and so I set out to find one for you, never thinking what a labor I had undertaken. You see the trouble is, in the way they tell them. I could find plenty of stories which were interesting, but the Turkish way of talking, which will do very well for people who are contented to sit all day sipping coffee and smoking, and listening to a story-teller, would not do at all for a lively young American who finds it hard to sit still five minutes.

Now, honestly, tell me how you would like this:

"There was once in Damascus a man by name ——— ———, with the honey of whose lips the poison of hardships was always mixed. Day and night he hastened like the breeze from North to South in the world of exertion, and was burning brightly like straw, from his endeavors in the oven of acquisition, in order to gain a loaf of bread, and to feed his family."

Isn't that a round about way to say that the man had to work hard to support his family? I knew you would cry out impatiently, and perhaps throw down the book, or at the very least, "skip."

Now, it grieves me to have one of you little people throw down my book, but it goes to my heart to have you "skip." I can't bear to give you a skipping book. So I thought, that although it was curious for grown-ups to read, this Turkish style wouldn't do for youngsters, and I finally found a story which shows the sort that are told in Turkey, but is a little more readable for you.

It is one of the original "Arabian Nights" stories, but is not always included in that book, and when found there, it is not quite like this. We will call it

ALI AND THE HAUNTED HOUSE.

Now listen:

"Ali of Cairo had inherited a fair property from his father; which he had spent in dissipation, and when almost destitute, quitting his family and native town for foreign parts, wandering from place to place, and obtaining the hospitality of old friends of his respected parent. He was passed on, as it were, from one to another, until at length he arrived at the gates of Cairo.

"He had but a few pieces in his purse when he halted there at sunset, just as the gate-keepers were closing the massive doors. He chatted with them as they admitted him, and in answer to their inquiries as to who he was (for they perceived by his language and bearing that his station was superior to what his shabby garments would have indicated), he cleverly insinuated that having ridden in advance of his own caravan to procure a warehouse sufficiently large for the large bulk of merchandise he had brought with him, he had been interrupted by robbers, who had stripped him to the skin, but had mercifully thrown him the worthless clothes he now wore.

"'By good luck,' said he, 'I found stuck in the grimy pocket of this robe a single piece of gold, which will suffice to yield us all a tolerable supper.'

"By this manœuvre, and by his affability and plausible frankness, he won both their hearts and their credence, so that the next morning he was confidently introduced by them to the Syndic of the merchants, as a plundered but wealthy trader, who was seeking to hire a dwelling-place and stores in that commercial city.

"His winning tongue and specious manners corroborated the story of the gate-keepers, and secured him the hospitality of the worthy trader. After the bath and dinner, the host bade his slave show his guest the two houses that were to be let, and to deliver up to Ali the key of whichever he might prefer.

"There were three ancient but well-preserved structures in a row, all of which were then unoccupied. Ali looked over two of them with a fastidious air, and then questioned the attendant respecting the ownership of the third.

"'That likewise belongs to my master,' replied the slave; 'but we no longer show it, for it is an unlucky house. Each tenant has perished the first night he slept within its walls.'

"Ali, however, persisted, and found the house more commodious and far more magnificent in its decorations than the two adjoining premises.

"'I will take this, and no other,' he persisted, for he hoped that he might thus be rid of his miserable existence, and the shuffling, scampish mode of living to which his necessities had driven him.

"'I may not let it to you without the consent of my master,' the slave remarked; 'but of course it would be for his interest to have it occupied.'

"They returned then to the owner's house, who, after some little conscientious denial, agreed to accept him as a tenant, upon his signing a paper by which he acknowledged his own cognizance of the danger, and exonerated his landlord from all responsibility. The latter, in the extreme of his good-nature, even lent the prodigal the necessary furniture for the night, and sent him lights and a comfortable supper.

"When he had performed the fitting attention, had supped, and then (for the thoughts of impending death had roused him to repentance for his past profligacy and present knavishness) prayed fervently for a happier and better life, should he be destined to survive the anticipated peril, he calmly laid himself down on his pallet in a superbly-fitted saloon, where he proposed to pass the night.

"Scarcely had he extinguished his candle when a lurid light

seemed to roll like a cloud toward him, and a mighty voice roared in his ears:

"'Ali, son of Hassan! shall I send down the gold?'

"Not a whit dismayed, for his fortunes were desperate, his answer was bold and prompt:

"'Ay; down with it, and the sooner the better!'

Hardly had he ceased to speak, when, hurled as it were from a catapult, the gold descended from the fretted ceiling in one continuously pelting shower, until the quantity was so vast as to endanger the stability of the flooring. Not any of it, however, fell upon himself, but the coins were piled in a vast, glittering circle all around him.

"'Now that my task is accomplished, dismiss me to my pristine freedom,' again roared the bell-mouthed voice, which shook the very walls by its reverberations.

"'I adjure thee, in the most holy name of Allah, that thou explain to me the meaning of this marvel.'

"'From distant ages the gold was stored for Ali, son of Hassan, and delivered to my charge by one of his ancestors, a potent magician, that I might render it up to him at his demand. Whosoever, then, has ventured here and been terrified at my voice, him have I slain. Thou, on the contrary, hast fearlessly claimed thine own, and to thee have I now delivered it. There is yet another treasure reserved for thee in the land of Yemen, and when thou shalt have journeyed thither it will be found by thee. And now, free me, mortal, from my servitude.'

"'Bring me that treasure likewise, and do me yet another service, and I will liberate thee forever.'

"'Swear it!' solemnly tolled the awful voice.

"'By him who framed the talisman which enthralled thee, I swear it! Gently bring hither my wife and children, so as to neither hurt nor terrify them, along with the other treasure thou hast spoken of, and henceforth thou art free forever.'

"'Thanks, mortal; I go to fetch them. In three days expect thy family in Cairo. They shall enter the city with a stately procession, so as not to shame thee (for all things are known to me), and thy Arabian wealth shall be brought with them.'

"And darkness resumed possession of the apartment, for the spirit had departed.

"The prodigal slept tranquilly till the morning, when he arose early and searched about the roomy mansion for a hiding-place for his golden heaps. Chance again favored him; there was a discolored slab in the flooring of the saloon, which was connected with a turning-pin, and which, by a peculiar pressure, could be made to slip away beneath the rest of the pavement.

"He had seen one of these in his old home; so, fancying the discolored slab might be movable, he tried the peculiar knack, and to his intense gratification saw the marble slide away, revealing to his eyes a capacious treasure vault, to which access was obtained by a narrow, winding flight of stairs.

"Driving on the great circle of coin toward the aperture, and then shoveling down the countless gold with both hands, he barely contrived to store away one-third of it before a loud rapping at the front door compelled him to withdraw from his energetic labor.

"Running to the street door, determined to bar all ingress to the saloon, he found it was only the slave with whom he had conversed the previous day, who, seeing him alive, gave a friendly nod, and hastened away to tell the glad tidings to his master.

"Harder than ever did he work to conceal his golden heaps from the expected visit of his host. The last coin was rattling down the vault, clinking as it fell, when the violent rapping at the house door announced the advent of the owner.

"With a vigorous haul the slab was again replaced, and the perspiring prodigal flew down the grand staircase, apologizing as he ushered in his visitor for his discourteous yet necessary delay.

"Unwonted toil and a dirty floor had not improved the general appearance of Ali, so that his landlord, after congratulating him on his safety, and inquiring whether anything disagreeable had disturbed his slumbers (to which question the tenant smilingly replied in the negative), dryly asked how long it would be before his goods arrived.

"'In three days, without fail; my caravan is too well guarded to be despoiled. Meanwhile, if I cannot get trust, I shall patiently submit to these filthy clothes, and these unfurnished walls.'

"Assurance begets confidence. The trusting merchant introduced him to his own tradesmen, and having related his story in the public bazar, presents of all sorts and from all quarters poured steadily upon him. His kind landlord even lent his slaves to prepare the house for the reception of his family.

"When the appointed time had come, the guardian spirit again appeared to the lucky one, saying:

"'Arise, and meet thy treasure and thy harem, which are within a few hours' journey of the city. Part of thy wealth consists of costly merchandise, the rich clothing of thy family was taken from it; but the mules, horses, camels, slaves, and escort are all genii.'

"Then Ali invited his friends and acquaintances to accompany him to his caravan, and requested them to bring their harems with them, that the women might be mutually introduced. So they all went forth together, and sat down to rest in one of the suburban gardens which looked upon the desert.

"They chatted and they joked, but from time to time gazed at the wide-spread sands. At last a dust rose like a moving column, then obscurely-defined groups seemed to emerge from it, and lastly these confused masses seemed to resolve themselves into clear and distinct individuals.

"The sounds of revelry, too, floated louder and louder toward them as the van of the cavalcade, with shout and song and dance, march joyously onward. The leader of the escort rode forward to our hero, and respectfully saluting him, apologized for the delay; and then the merchants on their richly caparisoned mules, and the ladies in their gilded litters, joined the caravan. The whole a stately procession, which, traversing the streets, slowly wound its way to the courtyard of the haunted mansion.

"Its new master received them all with the most profuse hospitality, and whilst the gentlemen were wondering at the vast array of chests which had been unloaded from the mules, the ladies were admiring the superb dresses of Ali's harem, suitable rather to Sultanas than to private individuals.

"Thus, in one short day, the fame of his wealth and importance was spread through the city, and the traders who had given him credit when in rags, prided themselves on their discernment.

"As Ali privately wished to dismiss the incarnate genii, he openly bade the leader of the caravan (the guardian of the treasure) to drive the mules and other animals that very evening a little space from the city, that they might be at daybreak ready to start on another journey.

"When night had buried all things in darkness, the genii, resuming their spiritual essence, were wafted through the sky to the realms of ether.

"Prosperity seemed to improve the morality of Ali, who, with every facility for indulgence from his almost illimitable wealth, never relapsed into his early wastefulness, and indeed became positively thrifty."

To really appreciate this story, you must imagine it told by a grave Turk in a turban, not in the comparatively simple language that you have read, but with all the flourish and big words possible to cram into it, like the little sample I gave you. Moreover, he often walks about while talking, and in some measure acts it out, so that it is more like a play than a story.

But now let us go back to the evening in the harem. If they do not have a story-teller, they may call in a minstrel, who will sing, and play some instrument, making up his songs as he goes along.

Or they may have a kind of Punch and Judy show, that is, a little play with wooden figures, though of course, the English ruffian, Punch, is replaced by one of the Turkish stamp. This is as popular with little Turks as Punch and Judy with you.

Sometimes the entertainment is furnished by a sort of clown, who says funny things, as our circus clowns. Sometimes by comic plays, or performing animals, as monkeys or bears.

The most valued entertainment, however, and the one they offer to distinguished guests, is the dance. Not that the hosts or their guests jump, or even glide, about the floor themselves. Goodness! what do you take them for? Fancy a solemn-faced Turk *dancing!*

The Turkish dance is quite a different affair from ours; it is done by professional dancing-girls, and is to look at, not to participate in. Moreover, even a hired dancer does not dance much, in Turkey. She postures, she makes gestures, she tells a story by her actions.

On page 51 is a dancer amusing the ladies in a harem. You see she has left her slippers on the edge of the little carpet or rug, on which she stands. In the corner, also, you can see another table, with a tray and dishes on it.

A lady who spent years among the Turks, in Damascus, tells of a dance she saw, where the dancer, a young girl, first told how she lived at home with her mother, how she went to the bazar, how she did the cooking and washing. Then came a change, and she told how her father wanted her to marry, and she did not want to, for Ali was fighting far away in the desert, and so on to the end of the story, all told by gestures and action, without a word to help.

One dance the same lady saw was a sword dance, where a graceful girl described, or acted out a fight, with a scimitar, which she whirled around her head and throat, under her arms, over her back, so rapidly, one could hardly see it, and within an inch of the guest's face, as if she were slashing at sixty enemies, dancing all the time to the queer, monotonous music.

When the entertainment is over, and the guests have gone home, the slaves come in and spread the beds on the floor;

everybody tumbles into one, and soon the whole house is asleep—thus ends the day for the little Turkish boys and girls.

I have told you how the Turkish boy behaves; perhaps you would like to know in what way the life of the Turkish girl is different. Until she is eight or nine years old, her life is about the same as her brother's; she goes in the street, she runs into her father's part of the house, and no restraints are put upon her.

But when she gets to be eight years old, she begins to feel grown up. When our girls are just getting interested in their studies, she leaves school, considers her education finished, and—puts on the veil!

That does not sound like anything very terrible, does it? But it is one of the great turning-points of her life. From that day she is no longer free to run about; from that day no man, except father and husband, when she has one, must look upon her face; no more may she go into her father's part of the house. Henceforth she belongs to the harem.

About this time her parents begin to think about her marriage, for she has nothing to do about it herself, except to submit to be married to the man, or rather boy, who is selected for her.

Perhaps you think that marriage has no place in an account of child-life, but it has in Turkey. There little girls are taken from their playthings to become wives, and often carry their dolls away with their bridal dresses.

A girl is married as young as eleven years, and a boy as young as seventeen. An unmarried woman or an unmarried man is unknown in all Turkey; it is considered a disgrace.

How do they go about it? Well, when a mother thinks it

TURKISH DANCING GIRL.

time her son had a wife, she sets out to find one for him. She starts on a tour of visits to her friends, and to any family where there are daughters old enough to marry. When a girl pleases her taste, she sits down with her mother for a business talk.

Fancy it, you young people, the two mothers arranging affairs! The girl's mother asks questions about the boy, and the boy's mother tells how much he will give his bride as dowry. If these matters are settled, the girl receives from the boy a gift of a piece of red silk, and some sugar-plums. When the mother returns she sends the boy a love token. A queer love token, indeed! one of the sugar-plums of which she has bitten off half!

The boy gives his bride her dowry, but the girl brings a trousseau equal to another dowry. Not only does this consist of clothes, as with us, but household furnishings, such as sets of bedding, furniture for two rooms, and kitchen utensils, curtains, carpets, and rugs.

A set of bedding is two mattresses, two quilted coverlets, and three bolsters; and a bride sometimes has as many as fifty sets; the kitchen articles are of copper, and very numerous; and the furniture, which you wouldn't think could be very much in such bare rooms, is divan covering of rich stuff embroidered with gold.

Besides this must be a handsome brasier, generally of brass, to hold the fire, and the house linen.

Then comes the child's wardrobe, which in Turkey is very costly. The wedding dress alone must cost not less than three or four hundred dollars (of course I am speaking of well-to-do families), and often reaches the sum of thousands of dollars, since it is embroidered with gold and pearls.

Then, of course, there are other dresses, several fur jackets, costly shawls, jewelry, and a thousand other things.

Dear me! Shall I try to tell you about the wedding? It lasts a whole week, and those two poor children must feel themselves thoroughly married when it is over.

The ceremonies begin on Monday with a procession from the bride's house to the bridegroom's, carrying her trousseau.

Should you like to see the bride in her grand array? Remember she is not more than eleven or twelve years old. In some parts of Turkey her face is a mask of gold-dust and gum (to keep it on), with spangles here and there, on the cheeks and forehead, and chin. Her eyebrows are thickly painted to meet, and her teeth are made black.

What a figure! poor child!

The whole of Monday is spent by the guests arranging her goods in a grand display. Clothes are hung around her room on lines stretched from side to side; jewels are kept under glass cases, and an arbor is made of artificial flowers, in which the bride is kept on exhibition.

Then the obliging guests go to the hall and arrange the rest of her property where it will make the greatest possible show; piles of bedding of silk, cotton and embroidery, and dozens of bright brass kettles and things.

This occupies all Monday night, and on Tuesday the bride is taken with great ceremony to the public bath, where she has to go three times around a certain platform, kiss everybody's hand, and be dressed in borrowed clothes.

On Wednesday the bride stays at home (her father's house), and receives the visits of the bridegroom's lady friends. Great ceremonies attend this, as everything else. Entertainments are provided, musicians, dancers, and other performers.

A curious thing happens when the guests are about to go. The bride is led to the door of the house, and every guest throws small gold coins over her head. Knowing that this will be done, a crowd of beggars and street boys are ready, and the scamble that takes place for the money is, to our notions, disgusting.

The only pretty part of the whole week's ceremonies takes place on this evening, when the entertainment is for the young girl friends of the little bride. Each girl takes a lighted taper and they form a procession with the bride leading, and wind about the garden, among the flower-beds, and through the trees. All are gay with bright-colored dresses, and adorned with jewels, with hair hanging over their shoulders, and as they go songs are sung and other music performed. It looks, to western barbarians, like a scene from fairy land, or a chapter out of the Arabian Nights.

But the night goes on and another curious thing takes place. You think the people must be sleepy by this time? Well—that may be so; but the wedding takes not only the days but the nights of a week.

This ceremony takes place toward morning, and is the application of the henna, which stains the ends of the fingers and toes a bright pink color, and is thought by a Turkish damsel to be very lovely.

The stuff is made ready, and the bride takes off her wedding finery. She then comes into the room shading her eyes with her left arm, and seats herself in the middle of the floor. Next she holds out her right hand, and some one covers it with a rich bath scarf.

Some one else plasters the scarf thickly with the henna mixture, and there the poor thing sits like a statue. Presently her future mother-in-law sticks a gold piece on to the scarf, where the henna holds it tight; after her come one at a time, each girl and woman belonging to the bridegroom's side of the house, and each one leaves a gold piece sticking there. I should think she must feel like a beggar.

But that's only half. The richly-covered right hand is now slipped into a silk bag, to be out of sight, and the bride changes her position. She shades her modest eyes with the right arm, and holds out her left hand. Now is the turn of her own mother and her friends. The same thing is done over by her side of the house.

The night is ended by staining the fingers and toes, and a last dance.

On Thursday the Turkish papa gives his daughter his parting advice and his blessing, while he puts around her waist the bridal girdle, and she goes to the house of her husband.

Here two days more are given to ceremonies too tedious to tell. They are mostly entertainments, feasting, drinking sherbet, smoking, music, and dancing.

Do you think I ought to tell about the bridal presents? Well, I simply can't, they're too many. Everybody gives, and everybody receives; and that's all I can say about it. Let us leave the poor little bride to settle into her new home, where her husband may already have a wife or two before her, for the religion of the Turks allows them four wives.

I told you how strange the outside of a Turkish house looks; how they are exactly opposite to ours, having the windows, and the balconies, the trees and fountains all inside, and only the back part of the house with its blank walls turned to the street.

The streets themselves, of course, are very different from ours too. They are narrow and dirty, and really only a way to get about in.

Besides their dismal looks, they are infested by half-wild dogs, which are always under foot, and always ready to snap at one.

I think you wanted to know, or I fancied you did, how the houses are warmed. Like the dinner-table, the stove is brought in when wanted, and is only a brasier with burning charcoal. Of course that does not go far toward warming their big rooms, and there is another funny contrivance used, though it is going out of fashion somewhat. It is called a tandoor, and is simply a frame covered with a wadded quilt which hangs down to the floor all around. The brasier is put under this, and every one who wishes, crawls under the quilt, having his head out, of course.

It's a comical sight to see a family enjoying the warmth of this queer stove when quite cold, a row of heads coming out from under a quilt; they look as if they had all gone to bed in a social way.

But sometimes it is not so funny, when one sets the clothes afire, as happens occasionally, or gets the head under the quilt, when the charcoal fumes soon put an end to life.

There's one thing at least, that is very pleasant among the Turks, and that is their kindness to animals. They have many of them as pets, birds, and lambs with spots of bright-colored dye here and there on their white coat, to make them more attractive. Then, also, they tame the various wild animals of the country, and in some parts of the country they have the Angora cat.

GETTING WARM.

Have you ever seen this beautiful creature, the loveliest of cats? It has long, shaggy fur like that of some dogs, as soft as swan's down, and a fine bushy tail.

If you've ever heard anything about Constantinople, the most beautiful city in the world (at a little distance), you have heard of the half-wild dogs that infest the streets. A few dogs would be useful, for the Turks need active scavengers in their streets, but there are so many that they have become a nuisance. They are under foot by day, and they make night hideous by barks and howls.

But they can't be thinned out by killing, because Turks dislike to take life of animals, and I read of a curious plan by which a few hundreds of them were carried off. A ship was hired, and by coaxing with food it was filled with dogs, several hundreds of them. The ship then set sail, went to a barren island at some distance, and by more food and coaxing, persuaded the dogs to go ashore.

When the last dog had landed, the ship quietly sailed off and left them to starve, or eat each other as they chose. That may have looked less cruel than shooting or drowning them to a Turk, but in our eyes it was a brutal act."

Before we leave the little Turk, let me show you how he looks when grown up, and become a soldier.

Is he not fierce with his terrible sword and tall hat?

SOLDIER OF TURKEY.

CHAPTER III.

THE OILED BABY; THE LITTLE SYRIAN.

THERE'S another abused baby in the land of the Turks, but it is not a Turkish baby, it is a Syrian. This poor little wretch is oiled!

A Syrian nurse thinks she knows more than old mother Nature herself, and she fancies that a baby is not ready to begin life in this world till she has had a finger in the business.

So she proceeds to finish the job by sticking her finger down its throat to clear the passage; then cracking all the joints to see that none have been left out (I suppose); and then moving all its poor little limbs around in a sort of gymnastic style, to convince herself that they are in working order.

After all this she goes on with the performance by washing it in strong brine, and then covering its tender body with a mixture of oil and basil, especially over the joints, so that they may never be sore; and at last the baby is wrapped up and allowed to rest.

That is, it may rest for awhile, but it must be oiled and powdered daily for many days, sometimes even for a month; and its wrapping up is something like the Turkish baby's. One long strip of muslin three or four inches wide, and ten feet long, is tightly wound around it from the neck to the heels, holding the restless little arms close to the sides.

BABY AND BRACELETS.

What for? Oh, because that stupid Syrian nurse thinks baby's bones are too soft to keep in place; or perhaps a little for the reason that it is easier to carry around a bundle, than a baby. She slings it over her back, or carries it like a stick on her arm.

It isn't much better off when in the cradle; for, like the Turkish baby, it is rocked all day and all night.

In some parts of the country baby is carried in a little hammock, made of some gay, striped cloth, and swinging over its mother's back; two little brown feet sticking out one side, and a little brown face, with a cap ornamented with coins, at the other. She can hang the tiny hammock over her forehead, and then she rocks the restless little fellow by swaying herself back and forth, and when he goes to sleep she can hang the hammock, baby and all, on a door-knob, or any other convenient place.

Here's one little man, on page 61, whose mamma has taken him out of his hammock, and who is enjoying something nice to eat that looks very much like a stick of American candy. This baby's mother is a bracelet seller, and sits on the ground waiting for customers with her bracelets before her, tied up in bunches like curtain-rings. See her necklace and her heavy ear-rings hanging down to her shoulders. She doesn't look much like our shop girls, does she?

But if you think she is ornamented, look at another woman of Syria. She has not only ear-rings and necklace, but heavy breast ornaments, bracelets, and armlets above her elbow. It is very likely that she carries her whole fortune about with her in jewelry.

But to go back to the little folk; there are great doings in the house, if the baby is a boy. (The way the Syrians receive a

girl baby I will tell you by and by.) Presents are sent in, and everybody calls to congratulate the family.

But the great event of the occasion is the preparation of a dainty dish made of pounded rice, spiced and sugared, and covered with nuts. Little bowls of this delicacy are sent around to all the relations. It is called mughly.

The Syrians believe as firmly as the Turks in the "evil eye;" so, of course, many precautions are taken to preserve the baby from it, which you will not care specially to hear.

You will be more interested in the songs they hear. Here is one to which the baby Syrian is taught to play "Pat-a-cake." Mr. Jessup gives it in English.

"Pat-a-cake, baby! make him dance!
May his age increase, and his year advance!
May his life, like the rock, long years endure,
O'ergrown with lilies, so sweet and pure."

And here's another, much like one of ours:

"Blacksmith, blacksmith, shoe the mare,
Shoe the colt with greatest care;
Hold the shoe and drive the nail,
Else your labor all will fail;
Shoe a donkey for Seleem,
And a colt for Ibraheem."

Now about the girl babies. When one is born no festivities are indulged in. There are no presents, and no dainties. The mother weeps, and the friends condole.

Why? One reason is, that a girl grows up and has to be married at some expense, thus taking property out of her father's house; while a boy brings a wife home, which adds to the family dignity. Another reason is, that a son will support his mother and the family, if the father dies. That is a stronger reason in Syria than it is in our country, for widows and young children are cruelly treated, and often brought to poverty.

Besides these, no woman, not even the mother, can rejoice in the birth of a girl, in a country where girls and women are abused, beaten, and brutally treated, and where no life is possible to them but one of drudgery and hard work.

No wonder the wretched mother weeps, and consents to have her girl baby put out of its misery.

But she does sing lullabies to her, if the child lives. Here is one, from Mr. Jessup again:

"Come, Cameleer, as quick as you can,
And make us soap from the green shenan,
To bathe our Lulu dear;
We'll wash her and dress her,
And then we'll caress her—
She'll sleep in her little sereer."

The *sereer* is the cradle.

There are many nursery songs, not all so nice as these, for Syrian mothers have a terrible fashion of calling down curses and misfortunes on every one who does not love the baby.

After hearing that, you'll not be surprised to learn that the children themselves use very bad language. When angry with another, a boy thinks nothing of calling down the most dreadful of evils on his playmate; and as for telling the truth, it is said to be impossible for a Syrian, big or little.

But there are pleasanter things to talk about in Syrian childhood. For instance, the plays; you'll be surprised to hear that those far-off youngsters play many of your games. Leap frog is one, and they call it "Owal howa." Baseball is another, and marbles, and Blind man's buff. Puss-in-the-corner, too, and Button, button, which they call "Pebble, pebble," and play with a small stone.

Then they have more playthings than the young Turk; some of terra cotta, such as horses, or donkeys with pack saddles, comical figures, and dolls, with arms and legs moved by strings.

Toy carts they have, also, and sugar birds and animals, which, like some other little people I have heard of, they make haste to eat up.

Then they are fond of singing as they play. They have a regular swinging song with a chorus, that their fathers and grandfathers sang before them. Not only the children sing; peddlers, and street people, all sing their wares. A man selling cakes and baked eggs, cries, in a sing-song tone:

"Ya karim ya Allah!" (O bountiful God) while he balances his big wooden tray on his head, and looks out for customers. And a tea peddler, with tea urn of boiling water, glasses, sugar and spoons, sings as he goes:

"Chai chai kiena cha-ee!"

Both these peddlers belong in Jerusalem, which, you know, is in Syria. All over the country the people sing-song their stories and their reading, and keep time by swaying their bodies back and forth.

That reminds me of their school, which you would laugh to see, and I'm sure a Syrian boy would stare at your schoolroom, with its benches and desks, maps and blackboards. His school is a bare room, where forty or fifty boys, leaving their shoes in a pile outside the door, go in, and squat down on the floor, each one holding his book, or tin card, with a lesson on it.

School begins! and what do you see? Every boy begins to study at the top of his voice, swaying back and forth, like a Chinese mandarin in the toy shops. When one goes up to the teacher to recite, he has to scream louder than the rest, to be heard at all.

Why, it's enough to make one crazy just to think of it, away off here in America, with a good broad ocean between us!

The teacher of this mad-house sort of a school has a long stick, with which he keeps the boys up to their work; and if one is unruly, he gets something more than an "error;" he is thrown on the floor, his ankles tied together, and he is beaten on the soles of his feet. This is no joke, I assure you.

If he is a very bad boy, there is a worse punishment for him. A chain is put around his waist, and some one walks behind him with a whip, driving him through the streets, and, worse still, making him kiss the hand of every man, woman, and child that he meets. If they wish to be very severe, they will stop where people are at work, and call out masons or other workmen, and make him kiss their hands.

You wonder what they learn at this queer school. They learn to read, and to recite prayers and other forms belonging to their religion, the Mohammedan. They learn to write—what! without desks?—Yes, indeed; they are quite superior to the need of desks. Each boy carries in his belt an ink case, and his paper he holds in his hand.

Here's a picture of a Syrian school, all out having their photograph taken, with the master and his stick to keep them quiet.

When school is dismissed, comes a grand scramble for shoes,

SCHOOL CHILDREN.

which are left outside the door, you remember. The first boy kicks over the pile to find his, and then comes a scene like one you may have seen, when forty or fifty American boys want the same thing at the same moment (a football, for instance). If a boy gets hurt, and one generally does, he cries out:

"Ya imme! ya imme!" which means, "O, my mother!"

He's a droll-looking youngster, this boy of Syria. He wears

WATER CARRIER.

red shoes, or slippers, with toes pointed and turned up, or yellow ones of the same style. When it happens to be wet or muddy, and he does not want to soil these gay colors, he mounts a pair of what he calls kob-kobs, but we should call little stilts. They are only a few inches high, and are fastened to a wooden sole, with a strap to slip over the toes; but they often slip, or turn, and then down comes the youth on his nose, and his kob-kobs go rattling over the stones, while he sets up a howl, exactly like a little far-western boy.

His clothes are as queer as his shoes. If he belongs to the common people, like those little water-carriers, he wears a blue bag, with two holes in the bottom for his legs to go through, which you might call trousers, a loose jacket, and a red cap. That is about all. His legs come through the bag nearly up to the knees; but he has no stockings, and often no shoes.

If his father is wealthy, he will dress exactly like the old gentleman, with white turban, and clothes of rich stuff and gay colors, not to mention jewels and ornaments, of which the people are very fond.

The Syrian girl is a copy of her mother, likewise, in silks and satins, embroidered and decorated, and above all, a veil! Here you see her on page 72. Even the girls of the very poor have a bit of common white muslin for this purpose, while the dress they wear is of coarse blue cotton cloth.

She wears her hair in braids, too, several of them hanging down her back; when she is grown up she will have many more braids, sometimes as many as twenty-five, and with every strand of every braid will be braided a black cord, to which are fastened little gold coins. This will hang down the back, sometimes to the knees, and it is, of course, very gorgeous. It will do very well for a lady who never goes into the street unless wrapped up like a mummy, or in the night, with a crowd of attendants

GROWN-UP GIRLS.

about her, to keep off the gaze of the vulgar; but wouldn't it be funny in New York? and wouldn't she draw a crowd!

GIRLS.

Their names are odd, too. What would you think of "Stuffed Cabbage" for a girl's name? or "Hotel," or "Civil War?" They are named after anything that happens to interest the parents at the time; and if a child gets sick, its name is changed. They think the name did not agree with it.

On page 71 are three of the grown-up girls. You cannot see the hair at the back, but you can see the strings of coins in front, and the veils.

IN THE COURT.

Their houses are different from ours; the wealthy build like the Turks, dead walls outside, and a beautiful court inside. Here is a picture of a part of a court, with its pond, or tank of water, and trees beyond. But the pleasantest part of the

Syrian house, when the weather is warm, as it is most of the time, is the roof.

Oh, what sport! I know you're wishing your mother would let you go on the roof, that most delightful spot on the place, to a boy.

But Syrian roofs are made to go on, and that's the difference. They are flat as any floor, and have generally a railing, or rather battlement around, so they are perfectly safe, and rather tame after all, you see. There the family sit in warm weather, and there they often sleep. Look at the little Syrian child's house with its flat roofs.

But I must tell you about the houses of the common people, the ordinary village house. It is probably made of stones piled together, but without mortar to hold them firm. For a roof logs are laid across and covered with earth a foot thick. And that is not the worst; it is often on a side hill, and sheep, and cattle, and donkeys walk right on to it and run about, and shake down the dirt on to the people below.

To be sure the people don't care, they don't trouble themselves for so small a thing as dirt!

Inside, the house is as curious as it is outside. To begin with, it is hardly high enough to stand up in. "If a man wants to stand up he can go out doors," the people say. At one end of the one room the floor is a little higher than the rest, with a trough around that part. That's the last thing you'd look for, inside a house, isn't it?

On the higher part the people live, and on the lower part the animals; cattle, sheep and calves, under the same roof with their masters, and they eat out of the trough.

The family mansion, or rather end of the mansion, is luxuri-

FLAT ROOFS.

ously furnished with mats to sleep on, a tray to eat from, and a few wooden plates and spoons. Of chairs they have no need, for there is the floor to sit on; tables would be too high, and as for bedsteads, they probably never heard of such a thing.

When this interesting family takes dinner, a tray is placed on a mat on the floor, and all sit around it. The dinner will be perhaps a camel stew, or a pottage, with olives and rice, or cooked figs, and it is set upon the tray, and every one helps himself, with fingers, of course, out of one dish.

For a lamp in the evening, this mansion is furnished with a saucer of oil, having a piece of wick lying over one edge.

When the mistress of the house makes bread, she heats her oven. This is not part of a stove or range, neither of these things does she use, it is simply a hole in the ground lined with plaster. She heats it by making a fire in it, and then sits down on the floor beside it to make, and bake, the bread. Her bread-pan is a flat stone, and on it she beats out her dough till it is flat as a pancake, and as large as a dinner-plate. This object she sticks on to the smooth side of the oven. It cooks quickly and curls up, but before it falls she takes it off, and puts another in its place.

I did not tell you all about the shoes these people wear. They are regarded as very unclean (as, indeed, they often are, especially boys' shoes), and they dislike very much to speak of them, considering it very impolite. If one is obliged to mention shoes, he will make an apology for alluding to so vile a subject. The reason they are left at the door, as they always are, is that everybody sits on the floor, as you see this woman with cushions and pipe, and houses are spread with clean mats for that purpose.

SMOKING.

But you haven't heard all about the children. They are managed when young, in the same silly way that nurses in our own country sometimes try, by frightening them, or at least making use of threats.

MOHAMMEDAN GIRL.

They tell them that the "Bahoo" is coming after them, to eat them up, or the "Bedawin" to catch them. And when you see what rag-bag looking fellows even the common peasants are—as you see in the picture—you can't wonder that they are afraid of a terrible Bedawin, who is supposed to be much more dreadful.

Then, too, the doctor, often the best friend the poor crea-

PEASANTS.

tures have, is held up as a terror, as he sometimes is in our country, by mothers who ought to know better. "If you don't be good the doctor'll come!" is a potent threat to the little Syrian.

The "manners" taught to the little man are somewhat different from any you are used to. First, he must always take off his shoes, and secondly he must always keep on his cap! When he enters a room with older people he must go around and kiss their hands, and place each one on his forehead.

I'm sorry to tell you a dreadful thing about them, that besides being extremely untruthful, they are exceedingly profane; and they smoke almost before they can walk, both boys and girls! See this little woman on page 78 with her pipe.

If one gets very angry at another he "calls names," as children do nearer home; but what is funny (to us) is, that he does not heap abuse on his enemy, but on his enemy's father, and grandfather, and great-grandfather, and great-great-grandfather, and the farther back in the history of the family he can go, the more insulting is he considered. Mr. Jessup, in his book about Syria, tells a story that would be laughable, if it were not so dreadful, of one boy hiding around the corner of his house to avoid the stones of an enemy, and shouting "and your great-great-great-great-grandfather!" and the other retorting as he ran, "and your great-great-great-great-great-grandfather!" always adding one generation more.

The Syrian girl, like her Turkish sister, is married very young, often before she is ten years old, and a week is spent in the ceremonies. She takes her dolls with her bridal outfit, and plays with them in her husband's house. Among other queer customs of that time in her life a bride is obliged to wear pattens, or a

AT THE FOUNTAIN.

sort of clogs, at least a foot high, on which she walks about the court-yard.

Another thing; the unfortunate little Syrian bride, remember she may be only ten years old! is not allowed to speak above a whisper till the "honeymoon" is past; still worse, she must go about with a handkerchief tied over her mouth till her mother-in-law takes pity on her, and tells her to take it off. To tell the plain truth, a Syrian bride is simply another slave to her husband's mother, and in any case is a hopeless drudge. She brings the water and carries the burdens, she grinds the corn in the hand-mill, and sometimes is yoked with cattle to drag the plow. She is beaten and abused, and insulted in every way. In fact, the life of a girl or woman in Syria has nothing to make it in the least desirable. Can we wonder that a mother sheds tears over her baby girl, or that she wishes her dead?

One rather curious duty of Syrian girls and young women is to fatten a sheep to be eaten. It is bought in summer, when pastures are burned by the sun, and sheep are very cheap. The animal is tied to a stake, and the girl sits down by it with a pile of balls, made of leaves and grass. She takes the head of the sheep under her arm and forces it to eat as much as it can possibly get down. It often gets so fat it can hardly stand, and at the end of four months is ready to be turned into fat mutton, and packed away in jars for use.

Some of the shops where little people go in Syria, would look very odd to you. For instance, a lantern shop. See what strange shapes the lanterns have, and what a roof! There's one thing in the picture that looks natural, and that is the little boy teazing a bird. I don't suppose a boy would be a boy unless he liked to worry something. Whether he wears a tar-

LANTERN SHOP.

boosh, like this one, or a fur mask like the little Siberian ; whether he's wrapped in a dressing-gown, or goes without clothes alto-

MOTHER AND SON.

gether ; whether he is white, black, red, or yellow, all the same he likes to teaze — doesn't he, boys ?

DEALER IN PEARLS.

Then there is the merchant of pearls, where the girls delight to go. See the strings upon strings of beads, and the shop-

GIRLS DRAWING WATER.

keeper, who turns his face away so that we shall not see it, and the woman in front, wrapped in her veil.

Besides the shops there are many sorts of peddlers, such as one who sells rosaries about the church. Here you see him

ROSARY SELLER.

with his goods spread out temptingly on the floor before him.

One of the sights for the children in Syria is the caravan of pilgrims to the Jordan. Some of the arrangements for making an easy journey are very funny. Mr. Warner, who wrote a book about this part of the world, tells about one that he saw. One woman rode in a sort of cupboard carried between two mules; some had chairs strapped on to the back of a horse, and others had great baskets or panniers slung each side of an unfortunate horse, in which a whole family could ride; a basket full of babies looked very pretty, though somewhat crowded. But the funniest looked like a sofa fastened across the horse's back, and four persons in a row, all facing the way they were riding, not lengthwise of the horse. It turned out to be not a sofa, but four baskets in a frame.

There's hardly a country in Asia where one may see so many different sorts of people, and so many different kinds of dress as in Syria. Here are girls who dress like boys, as these young Arab maidens, though to be sure, they are doing the work of girls, drawing water. See the queer, old-fashioned way in which they draw it, by letting down the jar by means of a rope. When the jars are full each girl will take one on her head, and walk off to her village without spilling a drop.

And then there are boys whose dress looks more like a girl's, as you see in the picture of the boy who has gone with his mother to mourn, on page 84.

There is also the great man, of whom the children are afraid, with his turban and full Turkish trowsers, who has power in the world, and looks fierce enough to bite the poor peasant standing like a beggar before him.

Then there are gypsies here as well as nearly everywhere else, and the girls often make a profession of dancing. Their dances are very unlike ours. One that I read of was performed by

POOR AND RICH.

two girls, and it consisted simply in whirling around each other, at first slowly, then getting faster and faster, till their long black hair stood out straight, and you couldn't tell one from the other; then suddenly the music stopped short, and the dancers fell to the floor exhausted. Here is a picture of a gypsy dancer with her tambourine.

The Syrians, big as well as little, are fond of dancers; on page 93 is another sort, with the musicians who play for it, covered with jewelry, and sitting on the floor like everybody in Syria.

These people are great story-lovers, and, as in Turkey, there are grown-up men who make a regular business of telling stories and singing, and playing some instrument. They go about to private houses, and to public cafés, where they are always well treated, and sure of listeners, old and young, and they get pay for their labor by what we call "taking up a collection." They are generally smart enough to stop in the most interesting place to get their money, and sometimes one will coolly walk off, and leave his story unfinished till the next day. That's something like our stories "continued in our next."

I will tell you a Syrian story, which Mr. Jessup has put into English for us.

It is about a flea, and before I begin I must tell you that this creature in Syria is by no means the insignificant object he is with us, confining his attentions to untidy dogs and cats.

He is, one may say, King of Syria. He actually drives the people out of their own houses, and they often desert a whole village, putting up some sort of a rude shelter in the fields for themselves, and leaving their proper homes to the little torments.

Now hear the story; I quote from Mr. Jessup's book, it is called

GYPSY DANCING GIRL.

The Noble Flea.

"A brilliant bug and a noble flea once went to the oven to shake off the ignoble fleas from their garments into the fire. But alas, alas, the noble flea lost his footing, fell into the fire and was consumed. Then the brilliant bug began to weep and mourn, saying:

"'Alas! ah me! the noble Flea!'

"While he was thus weeping, and his sad watch keeping, a glossy raven overhead flew swiftly down and gently said: 'O my friend! O brilliant bug! Why are you weeping on the rug?' The bug replied: 'O glossy raven, with your head all shorn and shaven, I am now weeping, and sad watch keeping.'

"'Over, ah me! the noble Flea!'

"The raven he, wept over the flea, and flew to a green palm tree, and in grief *dropped a feather*, like snow in wintry weather.

"The palm tree said, 'My glossy raven, why do you look so craven; why did you drop a feather, like snow in wintry weather?' The raven said, 'The flea is dead! I saw the brilliant bug weeping, and his sad watch keeping.'

"'Alas, alas! ah me! Over the noble Flea!

"Then the green palm tree, wept over the noble Flea. Said he, 'The flea is dead! and *all his branches shed*.'

"The shaggy wolf he strayed, to rest in the palm tree's shade. He saw the branches broken, of deepest grief the token, and said, 'O palm tree green, what sorrow have you seen? What noble one is dead, that you your branches shed?' He said: 'O wolf so shaggy, living in rocks so craggy, I saw the glossy raven, looking forlorn and craven, dropping down a feather, like snow in wintry weather. He saw the brilliant bug weeping, and his sad watch keeping.'

DANCER AND MUSICIANS.

"'Alas, alas, ah me! Over the noble Flea!'

"Then the wolf, in despair, *shed his shaggy hair.*

"Then the river clear and shining, saw the wolf in sorrow pining, asked him why, in sad despair, he had shed his shaggy hair? Said the wolf, 'O river shining, I in sorrow deep am pining, for the palm tree I have seen, shedding all his branches green;' and he saw the glossy raven, looking so forlorn and craven, as he dropped a downy feather, like the snow in wintry weather. He saw the brilliant bug weeping, and his sad watch keeping.

"'Alas, alas, ah me! Over the noble Flea.'

"Sadly then, the shining river, *dried its waters up forever.*

"Then the shepherd with his sheep, asked the river, once so deep, 'What great grief, O shining river, dried your waters up forever?' Said the river, once so shining, 'I in sorrow deep am pining, since I saw the wolf's despair, when he shed his shaggy hair, for the palm tree he had seen, shedding all his branches green; and he saw the glossy raven, looking so forlorn and craven, as he dropped a downy feather, like the snow in wintry weather. He saw the brilliant bug weeping, and his sad watch keeping,

"'Alas, alas, ah me! Over the noble Flea.'

"Then the shepherd, in sorrow deep, *tore the horns from all his sheep,* sadly bound them on his head, since he heard the flea was dead.

"Then the shepherd's mother dear, asked him why, in desert drear, he had torn, in sorrow deep, all the horns from off his sheep, sadly bound them on his head, just as though a friend was dead? Said he, ''Tis because the river dried his waters up forever, since he saw the wolf's despair, when he shed his shaggy hair, for the palm tree he had seen, shedding all his branches green; for he saw the glossy raven, looking so forlorn and craven, as he dropped a downy feather, like the snow in wintry weather. He saw the brilliant bug weeping, and his sad watch keeping,

"'Alas, alas, ah me! Over the noble Flea!'

"Mother sad began to cry, *thrust her needle in her eye;* could no longer see the thread, since she heard the flea was dead. Then the father, grave and bland, hearing this, *cut off his hand;* and the daughter,

STORY TELLER AND MUSICIAN.

when she hears, in despair *cuts off her ears.* And through

the town deep grief is spread, because they heard the flea was dead!"

Isn't that a funny story? Well, here's a picture of the teller. Some of their nursery stories, or rather, their children's stories, for they have no nurseries, are very much like ours. One in particular, is almost exactly like our story of the kids and the wolf.

You remember, of course, that the kids' mother left them alone at home, telling them to be sure and not open the door, except to her. The wolf, who was hungry, and very fond of kid for breakfast, came to the house, and after some time, by help of his wolfish cunning, made the three little innocents inside think he was their mamma, and open the door.

Of course you have not forgotten the catastrophe that took place, nor the speedy punishment of the monster. He swallowed the kids, and then being too full to get away, was obliged to stay till the mother got home, when she at once tore him open with her horns, and out leaped the three kids, as lively and frisky as ever.

The Syrian story is like this, as to events, but of course a wolf is not dreadful enough for their taste, and the thief in the story is a ghoul, whatever that may be.

Before we have done with Syria, I will show you a real Syrian village, set down in the hot sun. Doesn't it look like a toy village made of cardboard boxes?

VILLAGE.

CHAPTER IV.

THE BUNDLED-UP BABY; THE LITTLE PERSIAN.

NEXT door (on the map) to the little Turks, live the children of Persia, who begin their lives by hearing the profession of faith of their parents. We should think them rather young to be taught religion, but in the opinion of a Persian one can't begin too soon, so the baby's first sensation is the sound of the creed spoken in his ear. This makes him a member of the ranks of Mohammedans, and ready to begin life properly, in the opinion of his friends.

That is, after he is bundled-up; for this little fellow is another of the bandaged babies of Asia. From neck to heels is wound a long strip of cloth, that holds him still and makes him look like a log with a head on. Charms are then hung on him, or sewed to his clothes, to keep him from the evil eye; soon his head is shaved, and he is named with great ceremonies.

One ceremony is very curious. The father has a sheep killed, and its flesh made into broth, which his friends and neighbors are invited to eat. The bones, however, are carefully saved, and buried by the side of some stream of water.

The names are different from ours; they have no family name, but they often have a string of pre-names, and others, in a queer manner. For instance, suppose a man by the name of John, had a son James, and a father George. He might call himself

ON HORSEBACK.

"Father-of-James John son-of-George," and if he liked he could even make it longer by adding the place he was born, or the tribe to which he belonged.

School begins very young for the little Persian, for he has a good deal to learn and must finish by the time he is eighteen years old.

Like all the schools in Asia, this is very different from yours. The scholars sit around the teacher on the floor, and study aloud, swaying back and forth as they shout out the lessons.

If they're naughty they get a whipping on the soles of their feet, bastinado it is called. They learn reading, writing, arithmetic, astronomy, and a few other things, besides passages of poetry, and prayers from the Koran in Arabic.

Do they play? Well—yes; after a fashion. Their plays are a sort of practice for their grown-up days. They play with bow and sabre; they learn to be very expert with the dart, and to do anything on horseback.

If a boy is to be trained for the cavalry service, he practices all sort of gymnastics on a horse's back; to turn around in the saddle while going at full speed, and fire a carbine backwards, and to throw and catch darts.

In this picture on page 99 you see some of the performances the boys have to learn.

They have other gymnastics, also, in which they dance on their hands with their heels in the air, and stand on one hand alone.

In fact the life of a boy in Persia, is simply learning to be a man, and a grave, serious-looking little fellow he is in his queer dress, as you see him in this picture, where he leans against the wall in his father's court-yard, listening to the talk of his elders.

His coat, you see, is of the style so common all over Asia, the

IN A COURT.

dressing-gown shape. If he lived up just over the borders, his dressing-gown would take a little different style, like this youngster who looks so very wise in his sugar-loaf hat.

HOW THEY DRESS.

See what a curious string of dangling ornaments he has

over one shoulder. His mother and sister have beads and decorations enough for a wild African.

To return to Persia. What has the girl been doing all this time? She has been getting ready for her life as well as her brother.

Alas, her life will be spent shut up in a harem, and there's not much to learn; to sew, to embroider, perhaps to read and write, and to secure her own way, that is all.

You don't understand that last item in the education of the little Persian? I'm glad you don't; it is only taught to those who are under a despotic master, and who have to coax and cajole him.

Oh! the most important (in her eyes), I forgot to speak of, it is the great value of the veil! the terrible impropriety of showing her face.

You pity her? Well, you need not in the least; she would pity you.

"Poor little infidel!" she would say, if she knew about you and your ways. "She has to go about among vulgar crowds in the street, because she has to work, and has no one to support her in elegant idleness as we have!"

And if she knew that you eat your dinners at the table with your father and brothers, she would pity you still more, that you were not rich enough to have a table for yourselves, you and your mother.

As for her, nothing could coax her to do as you little barbarians do. What a good thing it is that we all like our own country and our own ways best.

The little Persian girl dresses like her mamma, in very wide trowsers of velvet or silk, and a muslin or silk over-garment, held in place by a girdle. When it is cold she wears a little jacket over this, and shawls. On her feet she has kid slippers with soles of ivory or wood. Her hair hangs down behind with pearls and jewels, or gold ornaments dangling from the ends. Over these, of course, she wears all the jewelry she can get.

When she goes out, she adds a long cloak and a veil, which makes her look as though wrapped in a sheet.

If she rides, it is in a takht-ir-evan, or a sort of litter carried by two mules. In this she can sit up or lie down, and it is very elegant, I assure you.

If she is poorer, and must ride, on a journey, for instance, she rides in a basket slung to one side of a mule. Another basket at his other side keeps the balance of things, and another person rides in that, with feet dangling.

Sometimes she rides on horseback, when she sits in her favorite attitude, like a Turk, on the animal, carrying her baby in a sling around her neck.

One of the Persian girl's greatest pleasures is to go to the bath-house, where there are always plenty of other girls and their mammas, and they can bathe, and eat sweets, and smoke, and tell stories, hours at a time.

The bathing is funny, one is rubbed and doused with pails of water, and soaped, and his joints all cracked, and at last rinsed and allowed to plunge into a tank.

Bathing of this sort, in public bath-houses, is one of the necessities of life to a Persian.

How to sit is an important thing for Persian little people to know. Before a superior they must sit on their heels, with their knees close together.

Perhaps I didn't tell you that these people, too, sit on the floor, or on divans, where they bring their feet up under them, as if on the floor.

Before an equal, the little Persian may sit with legs crossed, and his body erect. It is very rude to show the feet when seated, they must always be covered with the robe.

Going to bed isn't much trouble to these little folk. A mattress is laid on the floor, a pillow of down and a blanket on it, and that is all. If it is warm the bed is on the roof, if cold in the house, anywhere. There is no such a thing as a bedroom, as we understand it, in the house. Every one sleeps in his clothes, rolled in the blanket or quilt. The rich have their bedding of velvet or brocade, and the poor of cheaper stuff, but all alike sleep on the floor.

If one goes out in the evening he must carry a lantern, or have a servant to do so, and the bigger the lantern the more important the personage it lights. They are sometimes a yard high.

The best houses in Persia, at least on the outside, are for the pigeons. On page 106 is one near Ispahan. It looks like a castle, you see, but inside it is full of places for nests, and thousands of pigeons live there.

You've heard of Persian roses, no doubt, and this is the home of the rose. The bushes grow fourteen feet high, and have thousands of blossoms. Every house and garden has roses in pots, and every room has vases of them. Even the bath is strewed with roses, and on great occasions pools are spread with the blossoms, cut without stem, and arranged in various designs.

Other things grow besides roses; cucumbers six feet long, and two feet around, and melons so plenty, that horses are fed on them during the season; and so nice, that they are said to be the best in the world.

I told you, when speaking of little Turks, about the sort of stove the Persians have to keep warm by, and there is a picture

PIGEON HOUSE.

showing how the Turkish ladies enjoy it. But another curious thing in Persia is the bread.

KURDISH SOLDIER.

Bread—to a little Persian—means a big pancake, which comes in with dinner, and which he uses for plate and napkin, and then eats up.

His dinner he eats from the floor, without knife or fork; and, however elegant may be his home inside, on the outside it looks like a hovel of mud. The houses are almost entirely one story high, with nothing showing on the street but a wall covered with clay, and a low door.

You don't see why? Well, that's another thing in which the Persians are different from us; they are anxious to have the world think them poor, and we are anxious to have the world think us rich, at least, some of us are, though it is a silly wish.

Do you want to see a soldier of this country? On page 107 he is; a Kurdish soldier in the service of Persia.

The Persian baby begins life by being made a Mohammedan, you remember. Most Persians are of that religion, though they were once, long ago, of a different faith, and called by the outside world Fire-worshippers. There are still some of the old religion left, and they have what is called a Temple of Fire, as in this picture, where the fires never go out, and have not, for nobody knows how long.

Polite manners and elegant conversation are the principal things for the little Persian to learn. Literary discussions, and stories, told in the grandest sounding words, are the delight of the people. They will sit and smoke, and talk, talk, talk, from morning till night.

No matter whether they tell the truth, or keep their promise, or stand by a friend, they are always polite.

Stories they will listen to for hours at a time, and music they like when they don't have the trouble of making it.

TEMPLE OF FIRE.

See their curious musicians, and their still more curious instruments.

MUSIC.

Now I will give you a real Persian story, that the little people of this country have listened to with open mouth and eyes, many times, no doubt, and believed every word of it.

It is translated from the Arabic, and is called

THE LABORER AND THE FLYING CHAIR.

"There was formerly in Bagdad a curly-pated, avaricious fellow, who worked hard under an herb-seller, and by dint of penuriousness became possessed of fifteen golden deenars. He labored all day upon half a clove of garlic and a dry crust, then retired to his lodging, lighted his lamp, eat the remainder of his garlic and crust, placed before him his fifteen deenars, and amused himself with counting them over and over till the middle of the night, when he buried them under his mat, and laid himself down to sleep. This was his constant custom.

"One day he said to himself: 'I will walk to the caravansarie of Khulleel.' It happened to be Monday. He sat down in the square, when lo! a broker passed by, carrying a chair of wood, which he cried for sale at seventeen deenars. The laborer offered fourteen; upon which the broker said:

"'Give me earnest, while I consult the owner.'

He gave him a deenar; and the broker, after advising, returned and said:

"'Give me the money.'

"The laborer paid it down, and took the chair to his lodging, prepared his supper, lighted his lamp, examined his chair, and sat down upon it, but found no amusement in it compared to the counting of his beloved deenars.

"So the next morning he went to the market where the broker was standing. He began to abuse him, and said:

"'Tell me the properties of the chair, and in what consists its advantage.'

"The broker, much alarmed, replied:

"'I know not the properties, for I am only a broker, but come with me to the owner, and ask of him the virtue it contains; his was the profit.'

"The broker went with the laborer to the owner of the chair, who was a Jewish magician, to whom the broker said:

"'Tell us wherein is the advantage of the chair, or give back the money.'

"The jew replied:

"'The property of the chair is this: whoever sits in it must take a green switch in his hand and strike upon it, commanding it to convey him where he chooses; it will do so in an instant.'

"The laborer hearing this, said:

"'I have been wishing for such a curiosity as this all my life,' and ran as fast as he could to his lodging. When night fell, he seated himself in his chair, struck it with a green switch, as directed, and said:

"'Convey me to the terrace of the sultan's palace.'

"Instantly the chair ascended to the heavens, until he heard the angels singing their praises to God in the Milky Way. Then it descended gradually until it alighted on the terrace of the king's palace.

"The laborer descended from the terrace into a court, through a window of which he saw a light, and the door of the apartment open. He entered, and beheld the sultan's daughter lying upon a sofa like the full moon among the planets.

"He approached and kissed her hands, upon which, being much alarmed, she started up, and saw the laborer, a tall and brawny fellow, standing near her with a drawn dagger in his hand. With much trepidation she cried out:

"'Who art thou?'

"The laborer answered:

"'I am Izraeel, the angel of death, and am come to take thy soul, that of thy father, thy mother, their viziers, and those of their generals.'

"The princess hearing this, shook in her clothes, her hair stood on end, and she cried out:

"'Alas! alas! for what crimes dost thou come so suddenly upon us?'

"'He replied: 'It is solely on thy account; but if thy father will grant my request I will spare thine and all their lives.'

"'The princess said: 'Let me know thy wishes, for rather than die he will gratify a thousand.'

"The laborer cried out: 'If thy father will marry me to thee, I will spare him; but if not, I will instantly seize thy soul, thy father's, thy mother's, those of the nobles, the viziers, and the generals, in a single day.'

"The princess promised compliance, upon which he repaired to his chair, beat it with a switch, and said, 'Convey me to my own house.'

"It ascended as before to the sky; the princess viewed him mounting with astonishment, and believed that he was really Izraeel, the angel of death.

"She went to her mother and informed her of what he had said; the queen related the adventure to the sultan, who consulted his viziers, and told them of the threats of Izraeel, and his demand of the princess in marriage.

"The viziers exclaimed:

"'Save us, save us; if you make Izraeel your son-in-law the sovereigns of the world will bow down to your authority.'

"The sultan, upon this, sent for the cauzee and the witnesses, and immediately executed the deed of marriage for his daughter to Izraeel, the angel of death.

"On the following night the laborer ascended in his chair, and entered the princess' apartment, when she presented him the marriage deed, and said:

"'What remains now but to celebrate the nuptials?'

"Izraeel replied, 'I will not appear during the preparatory festivities, until the night of marriage, which shall be next Friday; so hasten.'

"Having said this he departed, and ascended in his chair in sight of the princess, till the height concealed him from view.

"While the usual ceremonies were going on at the palace, the artful laborer procurred a carpenter to fix over his chair a canopy of wood, in the form of a dome, which he covered over with green, yellow, and red silk in stripes, and placed all over it lanterns, in which he could fix candles.

"He then put on a green vest, and a crown set with pearls and diamonds, which he had stolen from the palace of the sultan.

"When the night of the marriage arrived the laborer sat down in his chair, placed his candles, and took with him a quantity of sulphur.

"Then he commanded the chair to ascend, and descend gradually into the court of the palace, where they were celebrating the nuptial ceremonies.

"The chair rose swiftly to such a height till the laborer could hear the angels sing; then he lighted his candles in the lanterns and gently descended.

"The sultan, the viziers, great officers of state, and the whole assembly now beheld Izraeel, the angel of death, descending from the sky in his green vest, and flashes of light (which he made with the sulphur) darting from the illuminated chair.

"Some days after the marriage, a cook-maid looking for something to light her fire, on the terrace of the palace found the laborer's chair, which she took away, broke up, and converted into fuel.

"At length, recollecting the machine, he wished to place it

safely for occasion, in the palace; but on searching the terrace could not find it; upon which, in the extravagance of his grief he tore his beard, cursed his stars, and scattered dust upon his head.

"As he dreaded discovery, he had now no resource but to slink from the palace under cover of the night, and retire to his former lodging, where he locked his door, wept and lamented his lost grandeur, till he was near perishing of hunger and thirst, and the fear accompanying the dread of discovery

["While in this state (to shorten the story), there appeared to him a "monstrous genius," who said he was a servant of the chair which had been exposed to the burning sun, and burnt in the fire. The laborer appealed to his sympathy with so good effect that——]

"The genius hearing this speech, and beholding the distress of the laborer, was deeply affected. He then gave him a cap and a ring, and said:

"'Take care of these, do not lose them, or thy life will be taken away!'

"The laborer took them, and said:

"'My lord, what are their properties?'

"'The genius replied: 'When thou puttest the cap upon thy head, thou wilt be invisible to all eyes; and as for the ring, when distress shall attend thee, press it, and I will come to thee instantly, and execute all thy demands.'

["Armed with these powerful objects the laborer returned to the palace, and was happy again till the viziers told the sultan their suspicions that his son-in-law was not the angel of death, but a common laborer, and suggested that his power be put to test. So the sultan pretended to be longing for fresh apples, though it was winter, and none were to be had. He sent for his daughter and asked her to request Izraeel to procure them. Of course this was very easy to the owner of a magic ring, and in a few minutes Izraeel presented the princess with a great quantity of apples, finer than ever seen in Bagdad.

"Other trials were made of Izraeel's power, the last of which was to disperse the army of an enemy which had come to destroy the sultan.

"Izraeel simply called for magical armor and weapons, from his genius of the chair, then put on his cap, and with the help of the genius went to the camp, and invisible themselves, killed so many of the enemy that they fled in confusion.

"They entered the tent of the prince, took him prisoner, and loaded his treasure upom camels belonging to him.]

"When the morning dawned, lo! the plain was cleared from the enemy; upon which the sultan ventured from the city to look for his son-in-law, Izraeel, whom he soon perceived advancing with his spoils, horses and mules and camels, heavily laden.

"The sultan was astonished to see only Izraeel among such a convoy, for the genius was invisible. He exulted beyond measure, and with his viziers, nobles and generals, bowing down kissed the ground before his son-in-law, and conducted him respectfully into the city, and seated him on the throne of his kingdom, which he resigned to him.

"Izraeel reigned, and lived happily with the princess until death the destroyer of all divided them."

How do you like that?

CHAPTER V.

THE BABY WITHOUT A HOME; THE LITTLE KIRGHIZ.

THERE'S one baby in Asia who never has a home; if he is found in one place to-day, he'll be in a different one to-morrow, or certainly next week. Never does he stay in one place more than three or four days. He's a Nomad.

What is that? That is a person who spends his life in wandering about, with never a settled home. His father is a Nomad, his mother, and all the family, and, indeed, all his race. He lives in a wide, high plain in Asia called the Kirghiz Steppes, where for two thousand miles one way, and twelve hundred the other, there is scarcely a town, and hardly a settled family.

Don't think he asks your pity, he abhors a settled life. He says that he is not so lazy as to stay in one place, that while the sun and moon, the water, and the animals all keep moving, he shall do so too.

It's well he likes it, for he could not easily live any other way there. His father has thousands of animals, sheep, horses and camels, and it is to find food for them that he moves all the time. If his father is a Kirghiz chief, he may own ten thousand horses, a thousand camels, and uncounted sheep, and since his family is so big, of course he can never have a neighbor.

No playmate can the Kirghiz youngster have out of his own family, except the calves and colts, with which he frolics; and no school is kept on the Steppes. The first thing he learns is to care for animals, and to ride.

To ride is almost the first thing that happens to him in the world. He begins in the cradle, which is strapped on to a camel before mamma, and thus he takes his first journeys. As soon as he is a little bigger, and can sit up, he rides in a bag fastened to the back of some steady-going animal. There are two bags on the animal, and two children as passengers.

But he soon outgrows the bag carriage; the next thing is to have an animal to himself, and this is generally a calf, arranged with a saddle, to each side of which is fastened a boot of felt. With his legs in these boots, of course the youngster can't fall off, and very grand he feels, guiding his young steed by a thong in the nose.

When he is bigger he will ride a larger animal, and at last will be a splendid horseman. When I say *he*, I mean not the boys alone, the girls are equally expert, and the boasted accomplishments of the daughter of a Kirghiz sultan were horsemanship, hunting with a hawk, throwing the lance, and wielding a battle-axe with effect.

The funniest thing about the little Kirghiz, is his dress. Of course it is exactly like his papa's, as is the dress of little people nearly all over Asia. It consists of a pair of wide baggy trowsers, and one or more dressing gowns over them. The trowsers are usually of yellowish-colored leather, though a Kirghiz dandy sometimes has them made of velvet, and elegantly embroidered in gay colors.

The dressing-gown is the great thing. In warm weather he will wear one of cotton or silk, and, as the weather gets cool, he will add one after another till he is bundled up in several of them; but when it is really winter, and such a winter, too, as you can hardly imagine, the outer dressing-gown, kalat, they call it, will be of fur. This very useful garment is made double, and, it is said, that when one side is soiled, the kalat is turned the other side out. This side growing even worse than the first, it is turned back again, and so it goes on, turning from side to side till it is in rags, and falls to pieces.

This is not a pleasant thing to say about the Kirghiz, but we didn't expect to find everything according to our notions, did we?

But our boy isn't fully dressed; when quite young he wears no cap, but as he grows tall, his head is shaved, and he has a tall sugar-loaf shaped black hat made of lamb skin, with perhaps a band of other skin on the lower part to shade his eyes. Then, too, he has boots, very elegant affairs of red, or green, or some bright color, made with high heels, and long turned up toes. The sole and all is of the same leather; so if our young friend wishes to walk out, he *puts on his slippers!* These are of some stronger material.

But the young Kirghiz needs a belt, which is usually a shawl, and a pair of immense sleeves to his kalat, so that when he wishes to be very polite, he can cover up his hands in them; for, queer as it seems to us, this is the height of elegance in the Steppes.

Shall we dress the little girl and her mamma? (for of course their dress is alike). Well, nothing is easier; they dress exactly like the brother and father, except as to the head. The girl has her hair cut off from the back of the head, and the front braided in many fine long braids. Over this she wears a sort of hood of white cotton or calico.

Here is a picture of a Kirghiz chief in his tent, with his daughter beside him, and his son in front of him. This is the house dress, of course.

HOME OF KIRGHIZ LITTLE PEOPLE.

It is hardly necessary to speak of the children and the grown-ups, too, for the whole race is said to be like a tribe of children. They are extremely fond of gay colors. The great desire of a man or boy is to wear a red velvet dressing-gown, and the women and girls indulge in silks, and satins, and velvets, of the gayest colors.

There's a funny story about this showy dress, too. The whole family in their moving about life, have to work. If the mother of the household is the wife of the richest and greatest chief, she has to take part in the milking of their many animals, and in the work of the tent. The men and boys, too, have their work in caring for the animals, and one would think there could be no use for velvets and satins.

There would not, in our way of thinking, but things in Asia are quite different. Mamma puts on her elegant satin kalat, milks, sets up or takes down the house (with help of her servants), mounts her camel or horse, and rides all day in her fine clothes, without dreaming that she is doing anything strange. Papa does the same with his.

The little people of Kirghizland, moving about every day or two, can never live in a house, or anything stationary; indeed, they are perfectly miserable inside of four walls, and feel as if they were in prison. Their home is a kibitka, a tent of felt over a frame, which opens something like an umbrella, and can be closed tightly, to move. On the next page is the inside of one; you can see the frame.

When the family wish to move only a little distance, six or eight of them can lift the house bodily and carry it off; but if they go far, it is taken down and packed on a camel, and one animal can carry the whole house.

The little Kirghiz never sleeps on a bedstead nor sits on a chair; he never eats from a table, nor is the proud possessor of a bureau-drawer; carpets there are in the house, that is, small carpets, like what we call rugs. Skins, and cushions, a few cooking utensils, and some great leather pails for milk, boxes of clothes, silks and such things, are all the furniture, even of the richest Kirghiz tent.

The beds are rugs or skins spread on the floor, and the young-

CHIEF IN HIS TENT.

sters sleep in their clothes, wrapped in furs and felt blankets. The floor is the table, and the dishes are wooden bowls. The dinner is cooked in an iron kettle over the fire in the middle of the tent, and if it is a whole sheep, as it often is, there is a kettle big enough to hold it, and an iron standard on which to place it over the fire.

The greatest, or the most important thing in the Kibitka is, perhaps, the koumis bag. Koumis is a drink of fermented milk, made by pouring the fresh milk into a leather bag of immense size, and every day drawing off what is wanted. It is the great drink of the people, and the first thing offered to a stranger. The people are so fond of it that they have small bottles to carry on the saddle when riding.

This picnic sort of life of the little Kirghiz may be all very well in summer, when the weather is warm and there's plenty of food for the animals; but there's a winter in every year, and winter is no joke on the Steppes of Asia.

It is so cold that one's eyelids freeze together, and the storms of wind and snow together are dreadful; tents are blown down, children blown out of their beds and lost in the snow-drifts; even grown people trying to walk a few rods have been blown so far away that they were lost, and could not find their way back through the blinding snow.

Then if no snow is on the ground, and if travelers or moving Kirghiz families are traveling through the sandy plains, the fearful winds blow up great clouds and drifts of sand, which cover and bury whole parties at once. When a sand-storm is seen on its way, both men and animals run for their lives; you can see them in the picture on page 125.

If they can get out of the path of the storm they are safe, if not they are buried. Such a storm coming toward a vast drove of horses and camels puts them all into a panic, and they gallop madly away in every direction.

There's another danger to the animals also. They are hardly

ever fed by their owners, and in very deep snows they often find it impossible to get enough to eat, and then they die in great numbers. A Kirghiz may be rich one day and a beggar the next.

Kirghiz boys and girls do not marry so young as the little people of India and other southern countries, but they are often betrothed to each other when very young. This matter is all arranged by the parents, and those most interested in the marriage have nothing to do about it till the bridegroom comes after his bride.

Then a funny scene takes place. The girl sits in a tent, singing, principally about sheep, for most of the Kirghiz songs are about that useful creature. Around her tent is a ring of the women of the tribe, gathered from far and near. When the bridegroom starts for the tent, where he has a right to go (for he has given his future father-in-law all the sheep he required for his daughter, and everything is settled), he is opposed by these women. They rush at him and beat him with sticks. Of course he doesn't enjoy it, but it is the fashion, so he goes on in.

There sits his bride, who at once makes him a present, a queer one too! some red silk, feathers and cloves. This is the regular bridal present to him. Now the women outside begin to sing, and a great feast is made. Friends come from everywhere, bringing sheep and horses to be eaten during the joyful time.

The big iron cauldron is kept over a fire boiling all day, and everybody eats as much as he can (and the amount a Kirghiz can eat is something fearful). Sometimes a hundred sheep and forty or fifty horses are eaten at one of these wedding feasts.

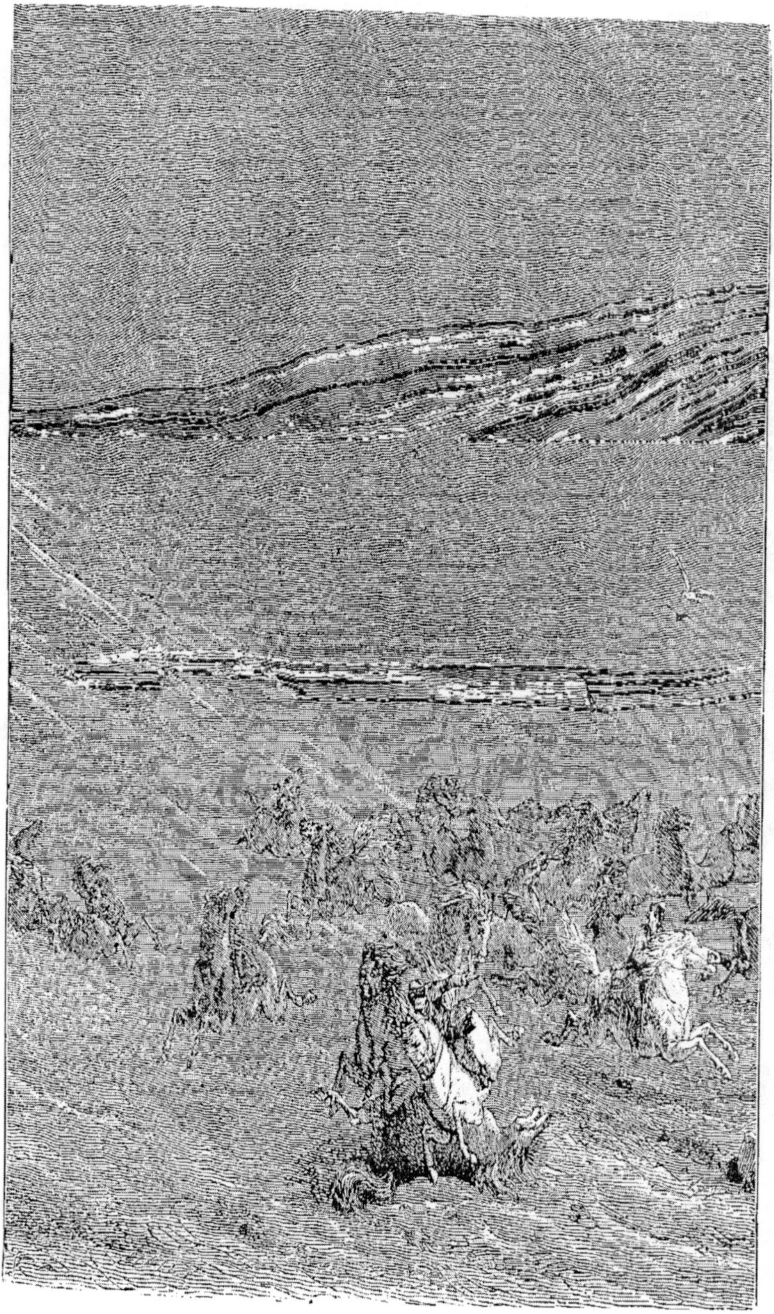

THEY RUN FOR THEIR LIVES.

After the eating come games, wrestling, and horse-racing, in the latter of which the girls take part, and then the young couple are considered to be married, and everybody goes back to his own Kibitka and his regular work.

The last thing I'm going to tell you about the little men and women of Kirghizland, will not, I hope, make you envy them

WHEN HE HAS A HOUSE, IT IS LIKE THIS.

in their wild, restless life; they have the biggest pockets you ever heard of! No amount of balls, and tops, and strings, and knives, and corks, and marbles, and mittens, and handkerchiefs, and nails, and other "traps" would overload their pockets, and call down a reproof and a solemn clearing out from mamma.

KIRGHIZ MUSIC.

Think of the delights of that, boys! and let me tell you how this wonderful pocket is made.

You know I told you they wear very wide leather trowsers; well, the trowsers are drawn around the waist by a string, and tied around the knee by two more strings, and the *whole inside is one big pocket!*

How dreadful! and yet how big!

The Kirghiz, like other people of Asia, are fond of music and story-telling. On page 127 is a musician entertaining a chief and his wife. Though he is a chief of his tribe you see he lives in a tent like the rest.

I told you the Kirghiz boy learned to be a good horseman. It's well he does, for sometimes he is surprised by a tiger, as you see here, and if he were clumsy he might not save his skin.

If a Kirghiz youngster ever does live in a house for awhile, it is not much of a building after all. See it on page 126, and it might about as well be a tent after all.

SURPRISED.

CHAPTER VI.

THE BABY WHO NEVER CRIES; THE LITTLE HINDU.

FAR away to the east of the little people in turbans and veils, live other youngsters, whose ways are stranger still.

I knew when we began this search into little folks' ways, that we should see queer things, but I must say, I did not expect to discover a baby who never cries, and here we have plumped right on to one!

"Never cries," say all the books, and yet there he lies, sometimes all day long in, or rather *on*, his cradle. Flies may torment him, mosquitoes may nip him, heat may burn him, and yet he rarely opens his mouth for any but pleasant sounds.

Worse still, if his mother is poor and has to work, he clings to her side, seated on her hip, and not only gets tired, but hungry and sleepy, and still the good-natured fellow does not cry or fret.

When he gets to be a big boy, and goes to school, he is good-tempered and patient; he rarely quarrels with his playmates, and even though a ragged street-boy, he is scarcely ever known to fight.

He does not lose this agreeable quality when he becomes a man; he is patient, good-natured, and polite, so much so that he is called the "mild Hindu;" for it is the boy of India that we're looking at now.

He is not perfect, he's no model—alas, no! He even has not some of the good traits that you American boys have. For instance, he has no idea of truthfulness. To tell a falsehood is not the unmanly, mean thing it is to you; to deceive people is not unworthy of him, as it is (or should be) to you. To the Hindu boy, what is the custom, and what will serve his purpose best, is thought more of than what is right. So it is with his father, so it was with most of the gods he learns about.

HINDU CRADLE.

This is not the only thing in which he differs from you; his whole life is as unlike yours as it is possible to make it. To begin with, he wears no clothes, to speak of, till he is several years old. His cradle, well, I wish you could see one! and you shall see a picture. Look at it! a square frame with a piece of muslin stretched over it, and hung from the wall by a cord at each corner.

On this swinging frame lies the black-eyed youngster, free to kick or roll, or tumble about as he likes. He is swung back and forth by his nurse or mother, and he is sung to sleep by a lullaby like this:

"Sleep, baby sleep!
Bread, butter, sugar;"

which is more senseless, even, than our own jingles.

This, you must know, is the well-to-do Hindu baby; many little folks in India have to do without the swing, I assure you.

BASKET CRADLES.

One that I told you of, lies under a falling stream, this is the Simla youngster; others ride in a basket on their mother's head, when she goes about, and lie on the ground when she works, as these from Northern India. Other young Indians are carried in baskets on the mother's back, as you have already seen in pictures, and still others in bags. There is one, a little gypsy baby—queer looking object it is too, its poor little head dangling

GYPSY BABY.

about, this way and that, till it is a wonder it does not fall off altogether.

HOME OF THE TODA LITTLE FOLK.

But what a looking father and mother! Gypsies are strange creatures wherever they are found, but these are the oddest yet, I think.

A TODA GIRL AND HER MOTHER.

When there are two youngsters to carry, the good-natured Indian papa will sometimes sling a basket on each end of a bamboo pole, put a baby in each one, raise the pole to his shoulder, and walk off as if he carried a load of goods, two loads, rather.

But these are all poor people, who have no settled home and nice swing for their little one, and so are forced to get along as best they can, without making any special fuss over him. As this one, for instance, the Toda baby, who is carried in his mother's arms and lives in this droll little hut, with a stone wall around it. You want to see this odd mother a little nearer? On page 135 she is made larger, with her daughter beside her. Interesting people, are they not? What a sulky looking girl! and what a dress!

That little fellow in the swing finds life a different thing. Queer doings about him, as you'll see.

The first thing is to clean house! Just at the time when *we* think baby should be kept warm, and the house quiet, the Hindu house is turned upside down, and inside out. It is cleaned from attic to cellar (or rather from roof to ground), or washed with mud inside and out, or sprinkled with holy water.

That'll do to begin; then everybody in the house must bathe and rub his head with oil, and all the friends of the family must come to a grand feast. I may as well say now, that nothing in the least important is done in India without something to eat. Now baby must be received into his caste.

[I'll tell you more about caste by and by.]

To perform this first duty the young Hindu is touched by the hand of the priest, who then makes an offering of bran and mustard-seed, to the God of Fire.

This will do for ten days, and then he must receive his name. This is a solemn affair, and the Brahmin (one of the priests) is called in to help. First he looks into his books to see if the planets are in a favorable position for the ceremony at the moment desired.

BRAHMIN AT PRAYER.

You don't see what the planets have to do with it? Well, you would if you were a Hindu. With them nothing is done unless the omens are favorable. If the signs do not suit, the Brahmin tries by prayers and sacrifices, to drive away the bad influence, and the day is settled upon. Friends and relatives come in, and baby is given a name, with the selection of which the stars and the month of his birth have something to do. Here is the Brahmin at his prayers.

All this time, you must know, the greatest pains have been taken to attract the "evil eye" away from the infant, by curious shells or coins, or any odd thing hung about him; or by exorcising with a little chaff and salt. Great care has been taken never to speak of the child at night, lest an owl hear the name, and repeat it, and the child should die! Nor to remark that he is healthy, or fat, or beautiful, lest some evil spirit should think it worth his while to make trouble.

Superstitious? Yes, it must be admitted our Hindu fellow creatures are so.

Above all things, now take heed! one must never, *never* pull a baby's nose! It will surely be ill.

And what do you suppose its mother would do then? Send for the doctor?—not she! She would fill a small earthen pan with rice and other things, and put in the street before her house.

What good would that do? Why, the first person who touched that dish, even accidentally, would carry off the disease, and baby would be well! At least so she thinks, and every passer-by believes so too, or anyway they step very carefully one side.

Other little folk of India live in boats. They belong to the northern part, to Kashmere, and the boat is thatched with matting, and has rolls of matting at the sides, which are let down at night, and so make a little more comfortable room. Here is a picture of one of these boats, with the side curtains up. When it can be rowed along the river everybody has a paddle,

THE HOME IN A BOAT.

down to the very baby; and when it has to be towed, as it often has, the whole family take hold of the rope.

In the picture the three, father, mother, and child, that you see pulling on a rope, are dragging their boat, which has not yet come in sight; but further up the stream you see another boat like theirs.

These boat people earn their living by carrying passengers up

THE KASHMERE BABY.

and down the river, and their pay is so small that they cannot hire help, so even the babies must work.

In the same part of India lives also this queer baby, who has her hair braided in many braids, with black cords braided in to make it look longer. See how long her hair hangs, and how

DRESS OF A CHILD IN INDIA.

different her dress from some of the other little people we have seen.

What is the woman doing on the ground? Not eating bread, as you may think. It does look like it, but probably she never saw a slice of bread like that. She is getting a piece of cotton ready to spin.

Over behind the little hill you can see the way they carry water, in a jar on the head.

To go back to the little Hindu. Six months now pass in peace over the roly-poly brown baby, while he grows strong and fat, and is kept from taking cold by a small bit of opium in his mouth now and then. Not a big piece, about half the size of a pea, but enough to give him a liking for it in after-life, and a dreadful thing, to our notions.

Then comes another great ceremony. Baby gets his first dish of rice, in the presence of all his friends and relatives, who have another feast, of course.

I haven't said anything about the fine things the baby wears all this time. Well, it isn't because he has none to wear, I assure you. He has no clothes as a general thing, to be sure; but, dear me! clothes are not needed! he's almost entirely covered with jewelry. Gold, and silver, and precious stones, armlets and bracelets, and anklets, rings and chains, and necklaces, as many as the parents can get together, are all heaped on to this one dusky baby. Poor fellow! Even the poor working people will manage to load their little ones with jewelry.

On the page back is a Mohammedan boy of India walking out with his mamma. He has no more clothes than the Hindu youngsters, but he is not so loaded with jewelry as they are.

Up to this time the Hindu baby boy, or Larka, and the baby

girl, or Larkee, have been treated alike. From this point their lives divide, and henceforth everything is different with them.

At three years of age comes the next important affair in the life of the Hindu boy, he has his head shaved. The priest, or Brahmin, comes, and likewise the tribe of friends, for another feast. The priest touches the boy's head with Cusa grass, in five places, on the back, the front, the top, and each side. Then the hair is shaved off, excepting a tuft on the back.

Now soon begins school-life. The boy, Chokra, he is now, has a muslin cap and coat, and begins his education. He isn't expected to play much, for both teacher and parents think that playing is the road to beggary. Parents like to see their children sitting quietly on the floor with arms folded, or taking a nap in the garden, and not, as we like best, to see them running about, growing strong and healthy by exercise.

His school [I speak of a native school, and not of those established by the English] his school is a queer place. It may be under a tree, or a thatched shed, where the ground is covered with sand, in which the young students can work their examples. Here they sit cross-legged, nearly all day, shouting lessons at the top of their voices, and swaying back and forth like the Turkish boy.

The exercises are something like this. They begin by singing an invocation to the God of Wisdom, and one would think they needed all the help they could get from him. Then come the lessons, which they learn by rote, or "by heart" as you say. An hour before the close of school, the scholars stand up in line, and hold their hands on their hearts while they repeat the multiplication table, the alphabet, and certain sacred hymns. At the end of each of these, they raise their hands to the forehead, and make a low bow.

The master then teaches them a long list of things they must do at home, and to each one they shout "Yes, yes." Then they prostrate themselves before the teacher, which is the same as your bowing, and all go home.

The funniest thing about a Hindu school is its punishments, for even these "good little boys" do sometimes have to be punished, and "errors" and "marks" would have no effect. If the boy has not been very naughty, he is beaten in the palm of the hand, something like our old fashion of feruling; or he is made to stand up and sit down a certain number of times, holding his own ears with his hands.

If he needs greater punishment, he is made to stand in some ridiculous or cruel position, perhaps bent over with one hand holding his toes, and a pebble on his neck, or something on his back, which he must keep from letting fall, or he will be beaten.

When the boy is about eight years old, if he is a Brahmin, comes the next great point in his life, putting on the sacred thread, which all of that caste wear.

By this ceremony the boy becomes what is called a "Twice-born" one, and he is considered a pure Brahmin, and fit to engage in any religious performances.

The boy is shaved, and a wire put in his ear, ready for an ear-ring. He is then bathed, and the sacred thread (the cotton of which has been sown, watered, gathered, spun and woven by Brahmins) is put around his body and over one shoulder, by the parent or some near relative. Offerings are made to the gods, texts from their sacred books are repeated, and various other religious acts take place during four days. It ends with a feast, of course.

Very different all this time has been the life of the Hindu Larkee. To begin with, she is met at the very first hour of her life with the question whether she shall be allowed to live. Not because they despise girls, as some have said, but because it is very costly to bring up a daughter. I will tell you why, very soon.

A son, moreover, will support the family, take care of his parents when they are old, and above all light the sacred fire that shall burn their dead bodies and hasten their departed spirits into a better state, and a daughter is not allowed in India to do any of these things.

What becomes of the poor Larkee who is not wanted in India? Well, the parents do the best they know, they do not mean to be cruel. They either put a bit of opium in the little mouth, and let her sleep herself to death, or they lay her in a little basket and set her afloat in the river Ganges, because they firmly believe that one who dies in that holy river goes directly to Paradise. There is not so much of this done in India since the English have ruled the country. In fact, many things are changing; but I am trying to tell you how the Hindus themselves lived, and how they still live where not changed by their rulers.

If the parents decide to let the poor little Hindu girl live, she has a pleasant life for a few years. She is shy and retiring, never boisterous like young American girls, and she is loaded with jewelry and sent to school.

I wish I could show you one of these little school girls. Her dress will be perhaps of gauze with threads of gold woven into the fabric. Her hair and ears, neck and arms, ankles and toes covered with gold and silver and precious stones. Thousands of dollars worth will be put on to one youngster of six, boy or girl.

Of course this is a great temptation to thieves, and children are often robbed in the streets.

HINDU DOLL.

One would suppose a child so dressed must belong to very wealthy parents, but the truth is, that often the whole fortune of the wearer will be in these things.

But let me tell you of another school-dress that I read of. It was a green satin vest, trimmed with gold lace, and a long rose-colored scarf, over white lower garments. What a gorgeous little school girl!

The Hindu girl has playthings. Of course she has a doll, and a droll object it is too. Here it is. It is made of wood, all dressed and adorned, and everything of wood. Nothing comes off but the head, which is held on by a peg. It is a gay object; nearly every color of the rainbow is painted on the clothes and ornaments. She may have a dozen dolls, of all sizes, but they will all be dressed in paint and gilt, with ears of a brilliant color, spots on nose and chin, and a head that comes off. Think of your dolls of bisque and wax, with their different dresses, and all to "come off."

But you needn't pity the little Larkee, she doubtless thinks her dolls the finest in the world, and dolls are important parts of the family in India. In wealthy families dolls have a room to themselves, are always sung to sleep, and enjoy as much attention as the children. Feasts and garden parties are given for them, they are married and die, and their little owners mourn as for a friend. I read an extract from a Bengal paper, giving an account of the marriage of two dolls belonging to wealthy Hindu families, where there was a grand street procession and expensive feasts to friends, and gifts to the poor, exactly as though it was a real wedding.

The boys too have toys. Elephants like those in our shops made of wood, and of all sizes, and the boys amuse themselves feeding them with rice, and giving them water to drink. Then they have also a cow (a funny creature as you see in this picture) and both are painted in the same gay style as the doll, with crimson and gold, dotted with yellow and blue stripes. Of these two animals the ears come off.

TOY COW.

The boys also have kites without tails, bows and arrows, marbles, tops, which they whip as you do, and they play jack-stones with five-sided nuts.

They have, too, games like ours: Puss-in-the-corner, Hide and seek, Blind-man's-buff, Odd and even, and others.

Many toys are made of silver, and of carved ivory for the rich, and similar ones of pewter and wood for the poor. The toy-peddler is a welcome visitor to the houses, and he has curious objects. Dogs with red heads and tails, blue bodies and black legs, horses, paper parrots, reed jumping-jacks, and lots of other things.

You'll be glad to know that the youngsters of India also know the delights of making mud pies, and they like to make figures of some Hindu god, and offer it sweetmeats of the same material.

Girls also embroider very nicely, especially little bags to hold spices, which they give to their friends; but the crowning toy for the girls is a live doll, or the child of some slave, which they adopt and play with almost as if it were a doll.

But little people grow fast in India, and about the time that your American youngsters are begining to go to Kindergarten, and thinking of school, the poor little Larkee of India is married! Truly; sometimes when she is not more than two or three years old. She doesn't go to live at her husband's house quite so young, not generally before she is eleven, but she is married with great ceremonies lasting five days, as early as her parents can make the arrangements.

It is a serious matter when her father sets out to look up a husband for her. That would be a serious matter in any part of the world, but the Hindu father makes it more so by the omens he is concerned about. If he should meet a dealer in oil, or a dog should shake his ears, or a crow fly over his head, or if any one of a thousand other things should happen, he would go home and try another day.

On the contrary, should he meet a young girl, flowers, or white rice, or elephant, or a dead body, a fish or a bangle seller, he would consider himself in luck, and go on his way joyfully.

When a husband is settled upon and the Larkee is betrothed, a veil is put on her (if she belongs to the aristocracy), the ends

HINDU MOTHERS.

of her fingers are dyed pink, and she is a *purdah nasheen* or "one who sits behind the curtain."

No more must her face be seen by any man except father, brother, or husband; no more may she go out in the streets except in a Palankeen, a sort of box carried by men. You need not pity her, it is her pride and joy. She is as proud of being a secluded woman as one of her sort among us is of living in grand style. It is aristocratic, it is the fashion, and the woman obliged to mix in the world as we do, considers herself one of the most unfortunate of beings.

Now her home is in the *Zenana*, or woman's quarters, and her boy betrothed becomes her playfellow. If he should die, even before the marriage ceremonies, she is a widow, and must never marry. Worse than that, she must shave her head, and become a slave and drudge to others, with no hope of ever being anything different.

Now begins her education, beyond what little (and very little it is) she has learned at school. Her mother is her teacher, and she learns cooking and religion! On the page back is a picture of two Hindu mothers.

You think that's easier to learn than French and music, and so forth, and so forth, that you have to learn? Wait till you hear; it is far from easy to a Hindu. Cooking is a serious matter, a part of their religion. Hindus are a marvelously religious people, they eat, and bathe, and dress, and marry, die and are buried, all according to their religion!

Every smallest thing about cooking and eating is done exactly as ordered by the law of their caste. The water must be brought from just such a place, in just such a way, and by just such a person. The food must be of just such kinds, and cooked in just such ways, and particular precautions must be taken to keep evil influences away from it.

A lower caste person casting an eye on any of the food or water, or even the shadow of such a person falling on it, defiles the food, and it is thrown away, even if the family go dinnerless. A stranger looking on a Hindu at his meal, defiles it. It is said one may go from one end of India to the other, and never see one of the higher caste eating. Many of them lock themselves in their kitchens to cook and eat their meals.

Most important of all, perhaps, is the manner of serving the food. The shape of the cloth, where it is spread, what dishes are used, and a thousand other things, are great and mighty matters to a Hindu.

To learn to cook the meals exactly right, and serve them in the same way, is one of the most important studies of the Hindu girl, and no matter how much money, nor how many servants a man has, his wife must cook and serve his food.

I have several times spoken of caste; I will say a few words about it here, although it is a subject too big for little people, not to say what it is for their elders.

There are in India four castes, and everybody is born into one or other of them. No power on earth can take a man out of his caste, or pass him to another. Every act of his life, even the very least, is ruled by the laws of his caste, and they follow him into the next world (in his opinion).

Brahmins or holy teachers are the highest, then kings and soldiers, third, farmers and traders, fourth, servants, besides outcastes, to whom belong the rest of the world. So strong a hold on the people has this institution of caste, that they will die rather than break its laws.

But that's enough about caste. I hope you haven't "skipped" it. Let us go back to the little Hindu girl, going on with her education under her mother's teaching.

When she has learned all the mighty and important matters about cooking and serving food, she is promoted to the study of religion, a queer study as her mother teaches it.

She begins by learning "by heart" many verses from their sacred book. Then come the histories of various Hindu gods, with dialogues, and mythical stories. Most important of all, however, is a certain quarrel between two of their gods, and their wives! This curious religious drama is carefully learned, word for word, out of a sacred book.

Besides being a religious exercise, it is a favorite amusement to act this scene, like a play, to entertain lady guests, while they sit around on the floor, in the Zenana, cracking and chewing roasted coffee, or otherwise having a social time.

When the Hindu girl knows all these things well, and is perhaps eleven years old, it is quite time for her to be married, if indeed she has not already been so.

Should her father allow her to reach the age of fourteen unmarried, he would be considered a most cruel parent, be despised by everybody, and degraded from his caste, which is a terrible thing I assure you, and it costs ever so much money to get back.

As for the girl herself she has nothing to do with it, except to obey her father, and be married to whoever he selects; nor does the boy have any more to say; it is all arranged by the parents.

The reason why there must be a law to compel the girl's father to marry her, is because of their curious way of celebrating a marriage. Marriage is in India the most important religious festival, as well as a chance for a social display. To make a grand and brilliant marriage is the aim of every parent, but this, naturally, is very costly.

The bride's father is obliged in the first place to make a great feast, to last for five days, to which anybody may come, friends, or perfect strangers.

Then there are processions at night, with torches, or lights, many fire-works, music and noise generally. Besides this he must scatter money among the people in the street, and let the crowd scramble for it. Rich men think it necessary to their dignity to throw away in this way sometimes two or three hundred thousand dollars.

You think perhaps the crowd would not scramble for it, but an Indian crowd would, eagerly. Beggary is respectable in that queer country. Brahmins regard it as right and even pious for them to beg, but a sin and disgrace to work, while the people believe that for every handful of rice given to a beggar he gets a certain amount of credit with the gods. The bigger the gift, the greater the credit, of course.

So a generous marriage display must fix a Hindu father all right for the next world, and it is well that it does, for it often ruins him for this world, since he goes into debt, and is unable to pay.

You see, then, why a girl baby is regarded as a luxury, and if the father has not a tolerably large fortune, he is afraid to undertake the marriage expenses which he cannot avoid. This is the reason that so many girl babies are quietly sent to paradise, by drowning or otherwise.

If, however, the father is not frightened, but spends his money liberally, he is looked upon with great respect, and the young bride goes proudly to live in the house of her husband, with a subject to talk about for the rest of her days.

What is that? Oh, her grand wedding! It makes her important for the rest of her life—poor child!

But the ceremonies are funny to us. The day before that fixed for the marriage, the bridegroom goes through some forms, to show that he has not neglected his religious studies. Then offerings are made, the last bit of hair is shaved off his head, and he pretends to set out to look for a wife. After awhile he plays that he can't find one, and then turns toward the river Ganges, as if about to go.

But a friend comes to the rescue, and offers to give him a bride, and the youth says he wants her now.

So he sets out in a gorgeous procession after her, the street people stare, and everybody is gratified, and he at last reaches the bride's house.

Now the two are seated together on a stool (which must be disagreeable, for they generally sit on the floor), and the priests repeat texts, and tell the names of their respected ancestors.

The next thing is to wash the feet of the bridegroom with water and milk! This doubtless means something; but outside barbarians can't be expected to know.

Next a yoke is held over the head of the bride, while the bridegroom repeats texts to her, and pours water on her head. Then he ties on her neck the marriage badge, which is a thin round piece of gold, always worn, and answering the same purpose that a wedding-ring does with us.

Dear me! this is a terribly long ceremony; how tired the poor things must be!

Then oil is put on their heads, and offerings are made, while more texts are repeated. Later, the two walk together around a fire, and touch a certain stone with their feet.

All this is on the first day, and it lasts for five days. Then come endless offerings, endless texts repeated, almost endless money scattered about, and plenty to eat for all the world who choose to come. Provisions from beginning to end. Every ceremony means something, and doubtless would be interesting as well as curious, if one could see them.

This is the regular marriage; and if it takes place when both are very young, as it often does, there is another ceremony when the bride goes to her husband's house, which lasts three days. It is of the same sort, though not quite so gorgeous as this.

This custom of early marriage is one great reason why Hindu girls can't go to school more. One just begins to get interested when she has to stop, and be married! Then comes the mother's teaching to fit her to be a Hindu wife, and after that the Zenana for the rest of her days, if (as I said before) she belongs to the upper castes.

She goes, like the Turkish bride, to the house of her husband's father, and is, in fact, the slave of her mother-in-law, if she chooses to have her so.

The house may be, and often is, even in well-to-do families, a poor place, without chairs or tables, with a rude short bedstead called a "Four-legs," without a mattress, a mat or two, a few boxes and cooking utensils.

But if the Larkee has married into a rich family, who live in great style, she will find the house built around a court, which is made as pretty as they can afford. All the house windows

IN A COURT.

look into it; there are trees and flowers, riding paths and fountains. Here is a picture of one, or a corner of one.

Queer doings are to be seen in these courts, the only "outdoors" the women enjoy. They ride horseback, with horses all decked with flowers and necklaces of big beads. Ladies and children, in silks and satins, for they never think of a riding habit, having the greatest fun.

Then they have bows and arrows, queer arrows, that whistle as they fly, and bows that throw little balls of clay like marbles.

But the greatest fun they have is with the swing. This is always as fine as they can afford, made of silver if they are rich enough, and hung between two posts. There's hardly a minute during the hours cool enough to be out of doors, when that swing isn't going.

Not even the rain keeps them out of it; indeed, it is their best loved sport to swing in the rain, and to come in all dripping. It is thought to be very daring, and quite an adventure. Fancy how dull must be their life.

Look in the house, and remember this is one of the finest sort. No chairs, not even a divan, as in Turkey. From one end of India to the other there was not such a thing as a chair (till foreigners brought them); from highest to the lowest, all sat on the floor, which is generally of stamped earth.

Carpets and cushions are considered furniture enough; a table a few inches high is brought in if wanted, and carried out again.

Sometimes they sit on their beds, but draw up their feet if they do. The bed of India is a strange affair. In a wealthy family its feet are made of silver, or gold, or ivory, while poorer families have them of wood.

It is a frame a foot high, with no head or foot boards, no posts, and no springs, but a bottom of broad tapes laced across.

But Hindus, you know, are fond of a swing, so sometimes the bed is hung from the wall, like a baby's cradle.

If the owner happens to be rich the bed is spread with velvet and satin, and the pillows, of different shapes, are covered with the same. Such a thing as a sheet or pillow-case is unknown. When the velvet or satin bedding is soiled, it is thrown away, and new put on.

It's a funny sight to see a grown-up woman sitting on the bed, perhaps with a lady guest beside her, and being swung back and forth by two servants, while a punkah boy outside pulls the string which moves the big fan, and keeps the room cool.

Still funnier is it to think of her being swung to sleep at night, or lulled by stories, just as was the Sultan in the Arabian Nights. The stories she likes are of warriors and heroes, fairies, enchantments, and sometimes adventures of the gods. The more marvelous they are the better she likes them, and many people believe every word of them.

PUNKAH BOY.

A servant or slave who can tell stories is valuable.

You needn't laugh at the women, you boys; the *men* of India are also gently coaxed to sleep by songs and story telling at their bedsides, in their part of the house.

You ought to see one of these families go to bed, though it isn't much to see, I must say. Perhaps the lady may lay off her outside jacket, perhaps not. Nothing else comes off. She simply lies down in her clothes.

How does the girl of India dress after she has gone to live with her mother-in-law? Silks, satins, gauze, brocade or velvet; these are the materials of her garments. She wears satin or silk trowsers, very wide at the ankle, sometimes eight yards wide. Then a close-fitting jacket without sleeves, and a looser one over. Sometimes an India shawl or two around her waist.

These clothes she wears till soiled, perhaps a day or two, perhaps longer if not very rich, and then throws them aside and gets new. Of the variety of undergarments which we wear she knows nothing.

Over the dress she puts on as much gold and jewelry as she can hang on. Not only rings on fingers and toes, and silver bells on her ankles, but bracelets away up to her shoulder, anklets of silver or gold, with jingling bangles and bells, chains on her neck, jewels in her hair, even a nose-ring if she is married (for it is a love token), and precious stones everywhere she can hang one on, or stick one in.

An Indian lady dressed up is a wonderful sight, I assure you; but I haven't ended the picture. The oddest ornament is the *tika*, a tiny gold cup-shaped object, stuck between the eyebrows with some sticking mixture, as you see in the picture on page 149, and the prettiest ornaments are the flowers, with which a lady will almost cover herself. She strings them on fine wire, and hangs them around her neck, or in her ears, or winds them around arms or ankles.

Her slippers, which she never wears in the house, are of gay-colored cloth, embroidered with silver or gold, and covered with pearls. Stockings she never heard of. Ah, children! what fun! she goes barefooted!

This you must remember is a rich lady, a *purdah nasheen!*

Common women wear one long piece of cotton cloth eight or nine yards long, which they throw over the right shoulder, and fasten around the waist. They can cover themselves entirely with this one garment, which falls in graceful folds. One end of it serves for a bonnet.

RESTING.

Parsee little people and their mothers, of which there are many in India, dress still another way, as you see here; girls and women who live in the mountains, and have to carry loads up and down, have yet another way of making their gay-colored clothes, and the queer boots to protect their feet from cold and rough walking, and boys and men who have to look after sheep dress very much like your old friend "Poor old Robinson Crusoe."

To tell the truth, it's rather hard to say how people do dress in that land of strange things, for nowhere are there more ways to cover the body than there.

But though she has but one garment, and lives in a mud hut, the Hindu women will generally be covered with ornaments. These things are almost the breath of life to her; taking them off is her way of going into mourning, and to show utterly crushing grief, she will pound up her jewels in a mortar!

MOUNTAIN BOOTS.

DRESS OF THE PARSEE LITTLE FOLK.

The Hindu man of the same rank wears two pieces of cotton, and a turban, with a pair of slippers or sandals.

Dinner is a curious affair in Hinduland. No cheerful table, with the family all around it; not even a dining-room. When a man wants his dinner he sits down on a mat on the ground, and his wife puts the meal before him.

That is the beginning. If the man is a Brahmin, the place prepared for him on the ground is square; if he was of a different caste, the dinner place would be triangular; if of another still, of round shape.

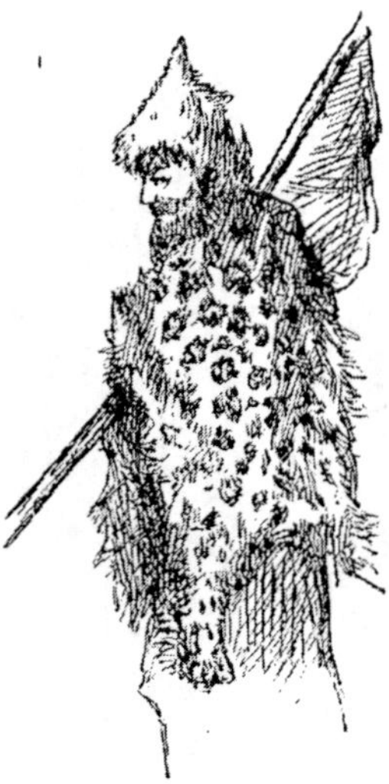

FROM THE MOUNTAINS.

He is seated; and now begins a scene. He bows to the dish that is brought in, lifts the plate in his left hand and blesses it, then turns his hand around the plate, or goes around it himself, in order to cut off all outside influence.

Then he offers five pieces to Yama, washes his mouth, offers five morsels to the five senses, wets his eyes, and eats his meal in silence, as quickly as he can.

He has neither knife or fork; he would scorn them. He thinks it very bad to use one of them a second time, for how can you know that it is perfectly clean, and has not been put to some other use!

But worst of all in his eyes, is our barbarous habit of sitting at a table covered with carcases and skeletons, as he regards the bones of our fowls and other meat. It makes him shudder with horror to see it.

His meat, when he has any, is boiled to get out the juice, and rice is cooked in that. So he gets the taste and goodness of the meat, without the horror of seeing it. His principal food is rice, with vegetables and fruits.

You think life in the Zenana seems dull? Where the mothers

THE PALANKEEN.

do nothing from morning till night but lounge, dress, decorate their children or themselves, amuse themselves in the court, or entertain their friends with the cost of their jewels; where they never read or sew, and where a woman will, for fifty years sometimes, never stir out of the gate; and if she does go, is covered up in a palankeen, like this, only shut up tight.

But there are amusements, even in private houses. There are the jugglers, who go about and perform most marvelous feats, such as, make a tree grow up, blossom and bear fruit from a seed they a short time before planted; there are the acrobats, boys as well as men, who do strange things with their limber joints; there are the minstrels, who play and sing long stories, and the regular story-tellers, who are always liked.

There is the toy juggler, a man who sits down on the floor with a box full of figures of people, horses, carriages, and other things, made of pasteboard apparently, scatters them around, and then begins to play on his tom-tom, or drum, when they all seem to come to life; the carriage jumps up into proper position, the horses take their places, the ladies arise and enter the carriage, and all is life and bustle, till the man stops playing, when, like a flash, they all fall dead as door-nails.

Then there are little girl jugglers, who do impossible things, such as roll themselves into balls, bend backwards, and pick up *with their eyelids* bits of straw stuck in the ground, thread needles with their toes, while their eyes are bandaged, and do any amount of dislocating of their joints.

There are the smake charmers, who will bring a basket of the cunning reptiles, and make them do as they choose, or charm others of their kind out of their holes by their music, which I'm sure wouldn't charm anything but a snake; and the tortoise charmers, who induce those seemingly stupid creatures to follow them about.

And there is always the dance! The dancers, called Nautch girls. are often sent for to amuse guests, and some of their

EGG DANCE.

dances are graceful. One that a lady guest saw in an Indian Zenana was a kite dance, in which the motions of flying kites were imitated, and a famous one is the egg dance, where a girl, holding a basket of eggs, fastens them one after another into little nooses in a circle of threads around her head, and then one by one takes them out again, all the time whirling around, and managing to do it without one egg touching another, or falling. This is a wonderful feat.

DANCING GIRL.

There are also the bird tamer, who makes his little pets sing, or fly, or run along his arm as he tells them to do, as you see here in this picture; and the peddler, whose pack is always mysterious to see, and often holds wonders.

Then for the little girl, whose mother is not afraid to show her face maybe a ride now and then in the carriage with this droll pair of animals to draw it. See page 168.

For the boy who goes into the street, there are many more things to be seen. There are festivals of all sorts, and processions without end, generally in the night, since that is the pleasantest time, and the moonlight is so bright one can read and write, and some writers say one needs an umbrella. These processions are brilliant affairs, with torches and music, and gorgeous display.

TRAINING BIRDS.

And there is the festival of light, when every house is illuminated; and the New Year's festival, which lasts four days, and on the last day, which is the New Year's day, the women sweep the house, collect the dust in a basket, put a lighted lamp in the middle, and throw the whole into the street, crying, "May sorrows and poverty go with you, and may the reign of Bali (that is, of prosperity) begin!"

HINDU PEDDLER.

It is rather interesting, that the day after New Year's is the day of Yama, and in memory of a visit he is said to have paid his sister, all Hindus go on that day to their sisters in the Zenana, and take presents to them.

Then there are the soldiers, to be seen on some great occasion, with their jackets of red velvet, and with plenty of gold and jewels, and their fine horses, covered with embroidered housings, feathers and fine saddles, and their manes braided up with silver ornaments. You see them on page 170; they even have bracelets on!

HINDU CARRIAGE.

But the soldiers are only the body-guard; a grander sight follows for the Hindu boy, who stares with all his might (if he's anything like an American boy), and that is a native king on his elephant.

A DECORATED ELEPHANT.

SOLDIERS.

Look at him. The elephant is painted, as you see, and decorated to the highest pitch, feathers, and fringes, velvet covering and bracelets (or anklets, would you call them ?), till he looks, as a traveler says, like a "mountain of gold sparkling with diamonds."

The *howdah*, in which the king sits, is made of solid gold, and the important person himself is fairly covered with diamonds. His servants on the footboard, hanging below his seat, wave peacock fans, and cloth of gold, and perfumes are

TRAVELING WAGON.

burnt before his steps. It's a very grand thing, altogether, more gorgeous than our western people can imagine, and more like fairyland than we shall ever see, perhaps.

Even these are not all the sights. The boy may travel, perhaps, in a covered wagon like the one on page 171, all wrapped in matting, and drawn by oxen. Then he will see the mail wagon, the stage we should call it, go rattling by, with its half-wild horses, and its English travelers.

MAIL WAGON.

And he will see the men drawing water by walking up and down the well sweep, while others carry it off in queer shaped

A JUMPING WELL.

leather pails, as you see here; or he may come across a strange and awkward fishing arrangement, like the one opposite.

If his journey is toward the city of Delhi, he may see a still

DRAWING WATER.

funnier sight, the jumping wells. These are quite large, often twenty feet square, and have high brick walls around them, perhaps forty feet above the water, like the picture on the last page.

But what are the people doing? That's what makes the thing funny; men and boys for a very little money, make a business of jumping from the high parapet around them into the water. Going down they throw themselves into all sorts of positions, and make up faces to be as droll as they can; but just before they touch the water they quickly straighten out, and go in feet first. You boys, who dive when you go in swimming, know

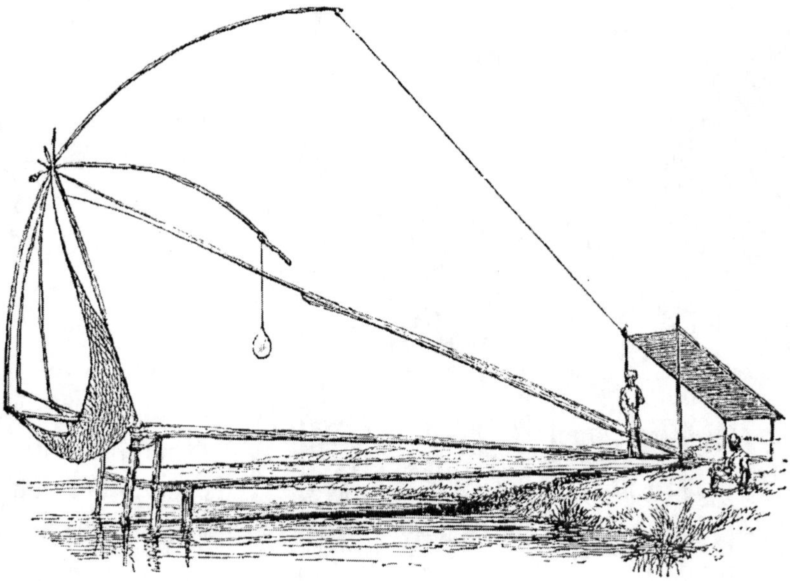

FISHING.

what a slap they'd get if they did not go in right. How would you like this way of getting a living?

Women carrying loads of tea leaves, in their big square baskets, is another curious sight in the mountains, where the roads are always climbing, and often so rough, that a fallen tree has to serve as a bridge.

These are the mothers of the babies I told you about before

who ride in baskets to the tea gardens. They belong to the tribe called Lepchas, and, strange as it may seem, little people are quite merry and happy there, though they live in the qeerest little houses, that look as if the first wind would blow them over. On page 180 is one belonging to a man who had plenty of money, and not to a beggar, as you might suppose. Besides money he had a herd of buffaloes, and ever so many other live creatures.

MOUNTAIN PEOPLE.

In this simple hut lived a very pretty girl, and growing over part of it was a passion flower vine, which in the proper season hung full of fruit, great golden balls as big as an egg, which are delicious to eat. Fancy eating the fruit of the passion flower.

But that's no worse than drinking the life juice of the palm, which the man in the pictures on page 181 is climbing up to get.

You see, he climbs by help of a sort of hoop around the tree, and around his body; and although it looks impossible to us, he does it easily, and as fast as you would go up on a ladder.

At his side hangs the gourd, which he means to fill with sap.

HOME OF UPPER CLASS LITTLE FOLK.

When he reaches the top he cuts a gash in the stem, and catches a quart of a white juice that gushes out. The next day he goes up again, and cuts a new place, and so he goes on till the season is over. In one picture you see he is nearly at the top The trees are often fifty feet high, and the man looks like a big monkey when he gets up there.

I have shown you two or three kinds of houses where the little people of India live, but they have been rather poor ones.

BRIDGE.

I will show you one more thatched hut, and then I shall show you a really elegant one, a palace, in fact.

On page 182 is the cottage, with its queer lattice windows, and on page 177 the palace, with beautiful bay-windows and balconies. Could there be a greater contrast? Yet there is quite as great difference in the people.

But in spite of its grandeur, there is one thing that looks

CINDERELLA

strange to us, and that is the lower story, which is furnished with awnings and a raised walk, and is apparently used for trade.

Now I want to tell you a story, one that has been told a thousand times in Indian homes, and that not only the children, but the women and the men also, will gather around to listen to.

But first you will be glad to hear that your old friend Cinderella is well known in India. Indeed, in one shape or another, that story is told almost everywhere. On page 179 is a picture of her as she looks in France. Should you like to hear how the Little Glass Slipper seems in Hindu dress? Listen:

HOME OF LEPCHA LITTLE FOLK.

"Once upon a time there was a Hindu Rajah, who had an only daughter, who was born with a golden necklace. In this necklace was her soul, and if it were taken off and worn by another the princess would die. Once on a birthday, the Rajah gave his daughter a pair of slippers, with ornaments of gold and gems on them. The princess went out upon a mountain to pluck flowers that grew there, and while stooping to pick them, one of her slippers fell off, and dropped into a forest below.

"A Prince who was hunting in the forest, picked up the lost slipper, and was so charmed with it that he desired to make its owner his wife. So he made his wish known everywhere, but nobody came to claim the slipper, and the poor Prince grew very unhappy. At last some people from the Rajah's country heard of it, and told the Prince where to find the Rajah's daughter. He went there and asked for her, and they were married.

CLIMBING THE PALM TREE.

ALMOST UP.

Some time after, another wife of the Prince, being jealous, stole the golden necklace, and put it on herself, and the Rajah's daughter died. But her body did not change, nor her face lose its bloom, and the Prince went every day to see her, for he loved her much, though she was dead. At last, however, he found out the secret of the necklace, got it back and put it on her neck, when her soul at once was born in her, and she came to life, and lived happy ever after."

Of course this is merely the outline of the story, but now I will give you one from a book full by Miss Frere, called "Old Deccan Days." It is

"The Brahmin and the Tiger.

"Once upon a time a Brahmin who was walking along the road, came upon an iron cage, in which a great Tiger had been shut up by the villagers who caught him.

ANOTHER HOME.

"As the Brahmin passed by the Tiger called out and said to him:

"'Brother Brahmin! Brother Brahmin! have pity on me and let me out of this cage, for one minute, only to drink a little water, for I am dying of thirst.'

"The Brahmin answered, 'No, I will not; for if I let you out of the cage you will eat me.'

"'O father of mercy!' answered the Tiger, 'in truth that I will not. I will never be so ungrateful; only let me out that I may drink some water and return.'

"Then the Brahmin took pity on him and opened the cage door; but no sooner had he done so than the Tiger, jumping out, said: 'Now I will eat you first, and drink the water afterward.'

"But the Brahmin said, 'Only do not kill me hastily. Let me first ask the opinion of six, and if all of them say it is just and fair that you should put me to death, then I am willing to die.'

"'Very well' answered the Tiger, 'it shall be as you say; we will first ask the opinion of six.'

"So the Brahmin and the Tiger walked on till they came to a Banyan tree, and the Brahman said to it:

"'Banyan tree! Banyan tree! hear and give judgment.'

"'On what must I give judgment?' asked the Banyan tree.

"'This Tiger,' said the Brahmin 'begged me to let him out of his cage, to drink a little water, and he promised not to hurt me if I did so; but now that I have let him out, he wishes to eat me. Is it just that he should do so or no?'

"The Banyan tree answered: 'Men often come to take shelter in the cool shade under my boughs from the scorching rays of the sun; but when they have rested, they cut and break my pretty branches, and wantonly scatter my leaves. Let the Tiger eat the man, for men are an ungrateful race.'

"At these words the Tiger would have instantly killed the Brahmin, but the Brahmin said: 'Tiger, Tiger, you must not kill me yet, for you promised that we should first hear the judgment of six.'

"'Very well,' said the Tiger, and they went on their way. After awhile they met a Camel.

"'Sir Camel! Sir Camel!' cried the Brahmin, 'hear and give judgment.'

"'On what shall I give judgment?' asked the Camel.

"And the Brahmin related how the Tiger had begged him to open the cage door, and promised not to eat him if he did so, and how he had afterwards determined to break his word, and asked if that were just or no.

"The Camel replied: 'When I was young and strong, and could do much work, my master took care of me and gave me good food; but now that I am old, and have lost all my strength in his service, he overloads me and starves me, and beats me without mercy. Let the Tiger eat the man, for men are an unjust and cruel race.'

"The Tiger would then have killed the Brahmin, but the latter said: 'Stop, Tiger, for we must first hear the judgment of six.'

"So they both went again on their way. At a little distance they found a Bullock lying by the roadside. The Brahmin said to him: 'Brother Bullock! Brother Bullock! hear and give judgment.'

"'On what must I give judgment?' asked the Bullock.

"The Brahmin answered: 'I found this Tiger in a cage, and he prayed me to open the door and let him out to drink a little water, and promised not to kill me if I did so; but when I had let him out, he resolved to put me to death. Is it fair he should do so or no?'

"The Bullock said: 'When I was able to work my master fed me well, and tended me carefully; but now I am old he has forgotten all I did for him, and left me by the roadside to die. Let the Tiger eat the man, for men have no pity.'

"Three out of six had given judgment against the Brahmin, but still he did not lose all hope, and determined to ask the other three.

"They next met an Eagle flying through the air, to whom the Brahmin cried, 'O Eagle! Great Eagle! hear and give judgment.'

"'On what must I give judgment?' asked the Eagle.

"The Brahmin stated the case, but the Eagle answered, 'Whenever men see me they try to shoot me: they climb the rocks and steal away my little ones. Let the Tiger eat the man, for men are the persecutors of the earth.'

"Then the Tiger began to roar, and said, 'The judgment of all is against you, O Brahmin.'

"But the Brahmin answered, 'Stay yet a little longer, for two others must first be asked.'

"After this they saw an Alligator, and the Brahmin related the matter to him, hoping for a more favorable verdict.

"But the Alligator said, 'Whenever I put my nose out of the water, men torment me and try to kill me. Let the Tiger eat the man, for as long as men live we shall have no rest.'

"The Brahmin gave himself up as lost, but again he prayed the Tiger to have patience, and let him ask the opinion of the sixth judge.

"Now the sixth was a Jackal. The Brahmin told his story, and said to him: 'Uncle Jackal! Uncle Jackal! say what is your judgment.'

"The Jackal replied: 'It is impossible for me to decide who is in the right and who in the wrong unless I see the exact position in which you were when the dispute began. Show me the place.'

"So the Brahmin and the Tiger returned to the place where they first met, and the Jackal went with them. When they got there the Jackal said, 'Now Brahmin, show me exactly where you stood.'

"'There,' said the Brahmin, standing by the iron tiger-cage.

"'Exactly there, was it?' asked the Jackal.

"'Exactly there,' replied the Brahmin.

"'Where was the Tiger then?' asked the Jackal.

"'In the cage,' answered the Tiger.

"'How do you mean?' said the Jackal, 'how were you within the cage? which way were you looking?'

"Why, I stood so,' said the Tiger, jumping into the cage, 'and my head was on this side.'

"'Very good,' said the Jackal, 'but I cannot judge without understanding the whole matter exactly. Was the cage door open or shut?'

"'Shut and bolted,' said the Brahmin.

"'Then shut and bolt it,' said the Jackal.

"When the Brahmin had done this the Jackal said: 'O you wicked and ungrateful Tiger! when the good Brahmin opened your cage door, is to eat him the only return you would make? Stay there then for the rest of your days, for no one will ever let you out again. Proceed on your journey, friend Brahmin. Your road lies that way, and mine this.'

"So saying, the Jackal ran off in one direction, and the Brahmin went rejoicing on his way in the other."

"There! How do you like a Hindu story? You see the jackal

THE WISE BEGUM.

is always the most knowing and cunning of animals in their stories, as the fox is in stories of other lands."

I want to show you a picture of a native Indian Queen, or Begum and tell you a little about her.

Here she is, dressed in her royal robes. You may not think she is very pretty, but if the old saying is true that "Handsome is that handsome does," she ought to be a beauty.

She was much in advance of the people about her, and by her wise government she improved her kingdom, paid off its debts, started schools and orphan asylums, stopped the trade in slaves, made roads, and in fact did her best to make her people more comfortable.

For ten years she worked twelve hours a day, living in a tent, and going about among the people.

Strangest of all, she began a revolt against women and girls being shut up in Harems. She never wore a veil, and brought up many young girls to do as she did.

Honors and praises were lavished on her by the English, and when she died, after ruling her kingdom of Bhopal nearly twenty years, her only daughter became Begum.

CHAPTER VII.

THE BABY IN DRESSING-GOWN; THE LITTLE THIBETAN.

People of the South do not have all the hard times in the world. There's another little fellow away up north, who spends half his life under a snowbank.

Think of that! From the time cold weather begins in the fall, till the spring's sun has melted twelve feet (or more) of snow, he never puts his nose, much less his toes, out of the house.

Nor does his papa! We might say the same of mamma, no doubt, if it were not for the yaks. If she did not go out every day and milk the yaks, and bring in the rich fresh milk to eat, how could they get along all that long, dreary winter?

You should think the father would do this work—I know; and *your* father would, but things are not the same all over the world, and in Thibet the women do the hard work.

So, as the Thibetan baby's papa is not obliged to go out, he prefers to stay in. This might seem rather queer to us, if we did not know something about the weather outside, which I'll tell you by and by. He is more comfortable inside, so he sits by the fire, and eats, and sleeps, and—spins!

I suppose he thinks it more manly to spin than to go out and look after the yaks, any way he does it.

Spinning is the great business of life in this family, especially during the long, dreary winter. Each one, children and all, carries a bundle of wool in his breast, and a spindle in his hand, and keeps them in use when not doing something else.

In the fall they made everything ready for winter; they got in their crops, made the curd and dried it, and hung bunches of hay high up in the branches of trees, so that when the snow was very deep some of the animals might reach it to eat and keep themselves from starving.

Then a good stock of fuel was laid in, and when it grew cold, and snow began to fall, so that the passes over the mountains were blocked up and no travelers could come through, each family shut itself up in its own low stone house, with walls four feet thick; doors were shut, fires stirred up, and what was one day a lively town of perhaps three hundred houses, on the next day looked like so many deserted mounds in the fast falling snow.

But every morning and evening the mothers come to the doors and call, "Toosh! To-o-osh! To-o-o-o-sh!"

Now Toosh, or the yak, is a sulky looking creature, who takes life very hard, and always looks sour. If she feels like it, when she hears the call she comes grunting and grumbling up to be milked, but if the idea doesn't strike her favorably she simply refuses to move.

That does not settle the matter; women who do men's work have manly accomplishments; *they can throw stones!* and what's more, they can hit every time. So say the travelers.

Well then, Toosh sometimes has to be reminded, by a stone against the ribs, that she is ex   to start, and then she comes up to be milked. When that is over she is dismissed, and wanders about with the herd wherever she chooses, getting to eat anything that is to be found under the snow, and never being fed by the people. No wonder she looks sour; life must be hard indeed to a Thibetan yak in winter.

But let us go into the house and see the little people. Enter a low door, go through a dark passage into a room nearly as cold as out doors, and dark as pitch. This is the store-room where food is kept, and fuel to keep the living room warm.

Into that room we climb by a sort of ladder, the rudest you can imagine, a mere notched stick.

No sooner are we in than we wish to rush out again, such a dreadful, smothering, foul place it is! Here in one low room are the whole family; eating, or smoking, but spinning of course.

Hold your breath a moment and look for the little ones. There are two or three dull looking children in dressing gowns spinning away like the grown-ups, and there's the baby. He looks contented, sucking away at some sweet morsel tied up in a rag.

What is it? sugar? No indeed, it's a queer mixture, to make baby brave. It is meat, dried and ground to powder, then mixed with fresh blood.

Ugh! let's get out of this! There are pleasanter things to tell about the Thibetan little folks, else I should never have mentioned them. Anyone except a native would prefer to be outside if he did freeze.

It's a good country to freeze in, too. Snow is twelve feet and more deep from December to April, and the winds are something terrific. Houses at all exposed have to be held down by big stones, and travelers die in great numbers.

Animals suffer too; horses have to be closely dressed in felt blankets, with their heads wrapped in furs. Camels and yaks are tougher, but they get loaded down with icicles that touch the ground, and rattle together as they walk.

They look very funny, as though preserved in sugar candy, as one traveler says, but they do not like it themselves. Sometimes a whole herd of yaks will be frozen in swimming a river. Huc, who passed through this dreary country in winter, saw such a sight. The ice was so clear that he could see the whole animal, and they looked exactly as if swimming; but they were frozen stiff, and had been dead a long time.

Other delights await travelers who visit Thibet in the winter. They can hardly get enough to eat to keep them alive, because everything freezes so solid they cannot bite it. Then the glare of the snow nearly blinds them. They have to wear shades, or spectacles of woven yak's hair. But the greatest thing is to keep warmth enough in their bodies to live. No matter how many wraps they put on, no matter how many coats and blankets and furs they have, they are all the time freezing their noses and cheeks, and what seems strangest of all they suffer intensely from cold eyelids!

Even the plants of the country are dressed in wool. Hooker, who gathered plants there, found them, with flowers and leaves, protected by great clubs of soft white wool; and the mosses are brittle as glass, and look like frosted silver; most exquisite they are, too.

No wonder the Thibetan buries himself in the snow, and never trusts his nose to those nipping blasts, and no wonder that baby has animal food; he needs it.

Buttered tea is a choice dish to little folks in these underground houses. Perhaps you would like to try the receipt. Here it is: Churn a handful of tea-leaves with salt, butter, and soda, thicken it with oatmeal, then boil it, and drink it down scalding hot. Then you can fancy yourself in Thibet, if you think you'd like it.

They eat other things, sticky balls of barley flour mixed with water, cakes fried in lard, cheese curd, parched wheat and corn, a few potatoes or turnips, and if very well-to-do, eggs, or chickens, or even yak's flesh. They eat little meat, and when they do they take it between meals, as we eat an apple. They never regard it as part of a regular meal.

To dine, is needed a dish or two, an earthen pot, a few wooden spoons, and a wooden cup, which every one carries in the breast of his gown for himself. There is little fuss about the meal, and no ceremony; every one helps himself.

But it is not always winter even in Thibet. Summer comes, and the country is covered with wandering Thibetans, who live in queer-looking black tents, which look like an enormous black spider, with his long legs sprawled out over the surrounding country. It is the ropes which hold up the tent that look like the legs of the spiders.

Around this tent the family will be seen, the father lounging on a pile of fuel by the door, the children without many clothes, crawling around, or perhaps burrowing like so many moles, the baby adorned with most of the wealth of the family, and the mother alone at work.

Or they will be met on the march carrying salt over the mountains, when every one that goes has his load. Yaks carry big ones, but sheep and dogs have each two little bags of salt, and every youngster that is big enough to walk has his load of salt too.

How do the youngsters dress? Well, just like the grown-ups,

in a sort of gown fastened around the waist with a sash, from which generally hangs a purse or bag.

To this gown the girls and women add a short sort of sack, and they wear their hair hanging in two long braids often fastened together in front. Lower class women wear a yellow cap, but great ladies (and there are great ladies even among the Thibetans) wear an elegant coronet of pearls.

These ladies do not wear a veil like most women of Asia, but they do what is worse, to hide their faces from strangers, they daub themselves with a sticky black stuff which makes them look hideous.

A queer headdress worn by some Thibetan women is a braid of yak's hair fastened to the back of the head, which stands out like the "glory" around the head of a saint; and another is a band across the forehead, from which hang coins and ornaments, down to the eyebrows.

If a man of Thibet wears a jewel, it is one ear-ring, in his left ear.

You have heard about some rather funny punishments for poor scholars, but the oddest is found in Thibet. A priest dressed in his robes (very gorgeous, too, they are, of yellow silk with sometimes red velvet boots, and mitre on the head) was hearing two boys recite.

He questioned them very gravely, and one answered pretty well, but the other evidently was a lazy youngster, and had not studied enough. So the master made him get upon his hands and knees, a cloth was thrown over his back, and he was supposed to be a horse!

The good boy then got upon his back, spurred, and kicked, and cuffed him, till he galloped around and back to the teacher again. Then the good boy got down, and questions began again.

They have some amusements. They make a great fuss over New Year's, beginning at midnight before, when a whole city breaks out into the wildest confusion, with music, and everybody goes into the streets, offering his neighbor a sort of dumpling to eat, which may be nice to a Thibetan, but is said to be anything but good to others.

Then on New Year's day there are great rejoicings, and children go about singing carols. They wear green robes, with little bells which jingle as they move.

It is amusing to see them sing, for they keep time like a pendulum, moving back and forth, but when they come to a refrain at the end of a verse, they stamp with their iron-bound shoes and sing with great spirit.

The reward they get is a little ball of butter, or a fried cake.

Of course the Thibetan baby is taught manners, and he salutes a friend in a way to make you laugh. For ordinary respectful greeting, he runs out his tongue; but if he wishes to be very polite, he uncovers his head and scratches his right ear at the same instant that he puts out his tongue!

What a sight must be the meeting of a party of friends!

These people, too, have a convenient way of sending presents to their absent friends, and to those who have passed away from earth. They get of the priests (lamas they are called) paper figures of horses all saddled and bridled, or of anything they think their friends would like.

Then instead of burning them as the Chinese do, they take them on a windy day to some high hill, and let the wind carry them away. They believe that Budha will turn them into living creatures and send them on their way.

The most curious thing in all Thibet is the "Feast of Flowers," a great festival which takes place soon after New Year's. It is a sort of a grand show of figures and pictures, every one of which is made of butter, as a modeler in our country makes them of clay.

There are hundreds of figures, colored like life, and so well, one almost believes they are real. All sorts of scenes, of people in different Asiatic dresses, animals, birds, and everything else; hunting scenes, scenes in the life of Budha, and in ordinary life of the people about them.

On the great evening, all these figures are displayed on framework near the convent, where they are made, for they are all arranged by the priests. The people come to see them, and to have a great time generally; they dance, and sing, and shout, and carry on wildly, and before morning every figure is smashed and scattered on the ground, and the three months' work of twenty priests is entirely destroyed. Queer idea of a good time, isn't it?

Another festival of the New Year takes place on the first new moon in February, and is a sort of masquerade. This is one of the funniest performances you can imagine.

First comes a dance by twenty-four priests, dressed up like various animals, as bears, stags, and others. After this is a dance of skeletons, or people dressed to look like them, who throw flour in the faces of the audience as they pass. When they are gone the animals come back, dance again, and six grave and dignified priests perform a great sacrifice, which ends the festival.

A THIBETAN PAPA.

The people of this strange country, not only the little people, but the big ones too, are firm believers in magic, and all sorts of witchcraft. Their stories, told around the fireside, show this.

Here is a story for you, taken from a collection of tales called "Sagas from the Far East." But first you must look at a picture of a Thibetan guide, as he travels over the country on his dromedary (on page 197).

"The Turbulent Subject.

"Long ago there lived in a district called Brschiss, a haughty, turbulent man. As he feared no man, and obeyed no laws, the Khan of that country sent to him, saying, 'Since thou wilt obey no laws, thou canst not remain in my country. Get thee gone hence, or submit to the laws!'

"But the turbulent man chose rather to go forth in exile than submit to the laws. So he went wandering forth till he came to a vast plain, covered with feather grass, and a palm tree standing in the midst, with a dead horse lying beneath it. Under the shade of the palm tree he sat down, saying, 'The head of this horse will be useful for food when my provisions are exhausted.' So he bound it into his waist-scarf, and climbed up into the palm tree to pass the night.

"He had scarcely composed himself to sleep when there was a great noise of shouting and yelling, which woke him up; and behold, there came hither toward the palm tree from the southern side of the steppe, a herd of demons, having ox-hide caps on their heads, and riding on horses covered with ox-hides. Nor had they long settled themselves, before another herd of demons came trooping toward the palm tree from the northern side of the steppe; and these wore paper caps, and rode on horses wearing paper coverings.

"All these demons now danced and feasted together, with great howling and shouting. The man looked down upon them from the tree top full of terror, but also full of envy at their enjoyment. As he leant over to watch them, the horse's head tumbled out of his girdle right among them, and scattered them in dire alarm in every direction, not one of them daring to look up to see whence it came. It was not till the morning light broke, however, that the man ventured to come down. When he did so, he said, 'Last night there was much feasting and drinking going on here; surely there must be something left from such a banquet!' Searching through the long feather grass all about, he discovered a gold goblet full of koumis, from which he drank long draughts, but it continued always full. At last he turned it down upon the ground, and immediately all manner of meats and cakes appeared. 'This goblet is indeed larder and cellar!' said the man; and taking it with him, he went on his way.

"Farther on he met a man brandishing a thick stick as he walked.

"'What is your stick good for that you brandish it so proudly?' asked the turbulent man.

"My stick is so much good, that when I say to it 'Fly, that man has stolen somewhat of me; fly after him and kill him, and bring me back my goods, it instantly flies at the man, and brings my things back.'

"'Yours is a good stick, but see my goblet: whatever you desire of meat or drink, this same goblet provides for the wishing. Will you exchange your stick against my goblet?'

"'That will I gladly,' rejoined the traveler.

"But the turbulent man having once made the change, cried to the stick, 'Fly, that man has stolen my goblet; fly after him and kill him, and bring me back my goblet!'

"Before the words had left his lips the stick flew through the air, killed the man, and brought back the goblet. Thus he had both the stick and the goblet.

"Farther on he saw a man coming who carried an iron hammer.

"'What is your hammer good for?' inquired he as they met.

"'My hammer is so good,' replied the traveler, 'that when I strike it nine times on the ground, immediately there rises an iron tower nine stories high.'

"'Yours is a good hammer,' replied the turbulent man, 'but look at my goblet; whatever you desire of meat or drink, this same goblet provides for the wishing. Will you change your hammer against my goblet?'

"'That will I gladly,' replied the wayfarer.

"But the turbulent man having once effected the exchange, cried to the stick, 'Fly, that man has stolen my goblet; fly after him, and kill him and bring me back the goblet.' The command was executed as soon as spoken, and the turbulent man thus had the hammer as well as the stick and the goblet.

"Farther on he saw a man carrying a goat's-leather bag.

"'What is your bag good for?' he inquired as they met.

"'My bag is so good that I have but to shake it and there comes a shower of rain, but if I shake it hard then it rains in torrents.'

"'Yours is a good bag,' replied the turbulent man, 'but see

my goblet; whatsoever you desire of meat or drink, it provides you for the wishing. Will you exchange your bag against my goblet?'

"'That will I gladly,' answered the traveler.

"But no sooner had the turbulent man possession of the bag, than he sent his stick as before, to recover the goblet also.

"Provided with all these magic articles, he had no fear in returning to his own country in spite of the command of the Khan. Arrived there about midnight, he established himself behind the Khan's palace, and striking the earth nine times with his iron hammer, there immediately appeared an iron fortress, nine stories high, towering far above the palace.

"In the morning the Khan said, 'Last night I heard knock, knock, knock several times. What will it have been?' So the Khanin rose and looked out, and answered him saying, 'Behold a great iron fortress, nine stories high, stands right over against the palace.'

"'This is some work of that turbulent rebel, I would wager,' replied the Khan, full of wrath. 'And he has brought it to pass that we must now measure our strength to the uttermost.' Then he rose and called together all his subjects, and bid them each bring their share of fuel to a great fire which he kindled all round the iron fortress; all the smiths, too, he summoned to bring their bellows and blow it, and thus it was turned into a fearful furnace.

Meanwhile the turbulent man sat quite unconcerned in the ninth story, with his mother and his son, occupied with feasting on the viands which the golden goblet provided. When the fire began to reach the eighth story, the man's mother caught a little alarm, saying, 'Evil will befall us if this fire which the Khan has kindled round us be left unchecked.' But he answered, 'Mother, fear nothing, I have the means of settling that.'

"Than he drew out his goat's-leather bag, went with it up to the highest turret of the fortress, and shook it till the rain flowed, and pretty well extinguished the fire; but he also went on shaking it till the rain fell in such torrents, that presently the whole neighborhood was inundated, and not only the embers of the fire but the smith's bellows were washed away, and the people and the Khan himself had much ado to escape with their lives.

"At last the gushing waters had worked a deep moat round the fortress in which the turbulent man lived henceforth secure, and the Khan durst admonish him no more."

CHAPTER VIII.

THE BUTTERED BABY; THE LITTLE TARTAR.

THE next queer baby in that land of queer things, is—buttered!

I'm not joking, it is a fact. For the first few days of his life he is kept covered with that greasy stuff. And, worse than that! when he goes out he is carried in his mother's boot. The oddest cradle we've heard of yet, I'm sure.

And mamma goes barefoot? Far from it! the boot is in its place on her feet; and what's more, she may have an older brother or sister in the other boot at the same time.

But the boots are different from ours; they are made of cloth, and the part above the ankle is big enough to carry a child four or five years old. Walking must be a funny operation (to see), with a youngster in each boot.

The cradle is not the only strange thing in this little fellow's life; in fact, it is just the beginning. As soon as he knows enough to hold on tightly to something, he is put on to a horse. At first it is behind an older person, and he holds on to his clothes, and takes his first lesson in riding.

This is the most important matter in life to him, for he's a Tartar baby, and a Tartar is almost a part of his horse. As soon as the youngster can hold on alone, he dispenses with help, and rides and practices so much, that at last it is impossible for a horse to throw him (without falling himself). Here are two of them on their pony.

So much of his life is on horseback, that he is awkward enough on foot; he is bow-legged, and his walk is something like that of a sailor on shore. His favorite games are played on horseback, he gets his wife in a horseback race, and he can sleep on a horse.

TARTAR BOYS.

The "manners" he learns are curious: that it is ill-bred to laugh, and undignified to move quickly. I don't suppose he would run to save his life. Then he must not spit on a fire, and it's a serious matter to blow out a light. To greet a friend in a polite way he must put his arm around him, and lay his chin on his friend's right shoulder, while the friend lays his chin on *his* right shoulder. Droll enough they look, too, to western barbarians, like you and me.

The walk he must cultivate, if he wishes to be elegant, is a waddle, an imitation of the gait of a goose! And to take his tea in a truly stylish manner is an art. The right elbow is

TARTAR SOLDIER.

placed in the left hand, the cup is held in the fingers of the right hand, and with one graceful swing is carried to the lips. Try it, and see how funny it is.

He learns something else besides manners. He learns to use

the bow and arrow, and the gun, and no doubt it is his highest ambition to get to be a soldier, and look like this interesting person on the last page in his fighting array.

TARTAR SCHOOL.

In the towns the boy goes to school, where he studies aloud, putting his fingers in his ears so that he will not be distracted by his neighbor's voice, and rocking from side to side as he bawls out his lessons.

See what a queer place is a Tartar school. The boys keep their hats on, and their shoes off; you see the shoes in a row in the front of the picture. On the column on one side you see hanging the school-bags, in which they carry their books.

The master does not show in this picture, but he sits a little one side on the floor, with a bundle of switches beside him; and if the boys do not behave well, and above all, do not study up loud and clear, you can guess what they get.

TARTAR GIRL.

See what curious ornaments on the walls, dragons, or some other imaginary creatures on the ceiling, and a suitable text or motto in the strange Tartar characters around the top of the wall.

How does this boy dress? He looks like a bundle of bed-clothes, and so does his father, and his mother, and his sister. Here she is. Pretty creature, isn't she?

The tailor is an unknown object to the little Tartar; his

mother makes his clothes as well as his father's, hats, boots, and all, and the shape of his coat is the pattern so much worn in Asia, the dressing-gown style.

The boy and his papa look exactly alike, except as to size; and an elegant dress for a Tartar gentleman is a silk kalat, or dressing-gown of different colors, a fine costly shawl around the waist, a tall cap turned up at the sides, and green leather boots, with overshoes or slippers to wear outside.

But if papa looks like a bundle of bedding, mamma looks even worse. You must know that it is very vulgar for a lady to go out at all in a city. Ladies of rank are never seen in public places, and those who have to go into the streets disguise themselves so that their own mothers wouldn't know them. They muffle themselves up in a big cloak, with the empty sleeves hanging down outside, and then wear a veil of horsehair over the face.

Well what *do* you suppose Tartar boys do for pockets? for not one do they have in their clumsy double-gown sort of garments. They use the folds of their gown, and they manage to stow away plenty of things there too. I have even read of cooking utensils and eatables carried there. As if your father should carry a frying-pan and a coffee-pot around with him.

There's one thing in which a Tartar youngster will beat the world, at least of his size, and that is in eating. He is particularly fond of fat and grease, and a regular drink is melted butter. It must be that the buttering he got in babyhood was to "form his taste."

A Tartar boy was once noticed (by a traveler) picking up bits of tallow that had dropped from the candle, and eating them as you would eat bits of sugar. He thought he would see how much the child would eat (he was about five years old), so he gave him a whole candle.

The boy was delighted! he munched it down as though it was a stick of candy, and looked for more. The gentleman gave him another candle; he ate that; then a third, and he finished that. The host began to regard this as a somewhat expensive treat, so the next gift was a lot of several pounds of sour, frozen butter, about the most dreadful stuff you can think of. The Tartar boy doted on butter, and he ate it greedily, as though the candles that had gone before were only to begin with. The traveler was bound to settle him at last, so he offered him a large piece of yellow soap.

He refused it you think? Indeed he did not; he ate it, every crumb, and was ready for more! What a horrible boy! But his father sets him the example. Monstrous stories are told of the quantity of meat a Tartar will eat at once.

I haven't told you how they live. Most of them spend their lives in tents, traveling from one place to another, and they often have thousands of cattle and horses to care for, since their wealth is in animals.

When they move to a new place, the tent is taken down, everything packed on to camels, and away they go; men and big boys on horseback, women and little folk on camels. Sometimes the camel that carries this load has two big baskets slung to his sides, in which mamma and the babies ride, but better is a big round sort of box, padded and stuffed to be comfortable, and set up like a big nest on a huge camel. In this the little ones can run about, or rather walk about, and not fall out, as the sides are high, and the mother herself can change her position if she likes.

By the way, though the camel is a four-footed baby he's an interesting fellow, and you may like to hear a little about him. In the first place he's perhaps the ugliest looking youngster in the world. He is tall and awkward, all legs and big black eyes a "wabbly" neck and almost no body at all. He can't stand up and he is never playful, as are all other young creatures, from a kitten to an elephant. No; the camel baby takes life as seriously as his mamma, and life always is a serious affair to a camel.

His training begins before he's a month old, by teaching him to bear light loads, and he gets on well enough following his mother, and living principally on milk, till he reaches his first birthday; then comes a change.

On the day he is one year old, the little camel's master announces to him that he must turn over a new leaf. He solemnly boxes the youngster's ears, and says:

"Henceforth thou drinkest no drop of milk," and the baby is a baby no more; he must eat with the grown-ups.

You hardly suspect so large and solemn an animal of being a cry-baby, but the camel deserves the name. If one is overloaded, or gets tired, he will cry in a shrill, human sort of a way that is unpleasant to hear; and if a camel's baby is taken away or dies, she will shed tears as well as howl over it.

These queer people have a funny way of treating the horses of which they are so fond. They keep them saddled, and tightly girt, day and night, and many of them will not let their horses lie down. They say if a horse lies down the corn he eats will settle in his legs and feet and make him lame.

When he is put in the stable he is covered from head to tail with several thick cloths, even in the hottest weather.

The wandering Tartars, who spend their lives in a tent, feel that a room is a prison. So when they are obliged to go into

INSIDE THE TENT.

a country more civilized than their own, and have to stay at a hotel, they pitch their tent as if on the desert, tie their animals around, and cook and eat as they are accustomed to do. They can't be happy under a roof.

Perhaps you think a tent cannot be very comfortable, but look

TARTAR DANCER.

at this one. You see it is as convenient as a room in a house. It has rich carpets, silk curtains, cushions and ornaments, and a window in the top. (See page 211.)

I must tell you of a favorite game in Tartary, played by the grown-up Tartar boy. It is all on horseback of course. The body of a goat is put on the ground, and the object is to pick it up without leaving the saddle, and then to keep it from all the other players who are trying to snatch it away.

It is wonderful to see how they ride without touching the bridle, wrestling with three or four for the prize, jumping banks and ditches, dodging and twisting about, and never falling off.

A great amusement here too, is the dance, where hired performers entertain the guests. See this evening party in the house of a rich Tartar. (Page 212.)

But of course the main entertainment of a Tartar's life is smoking. Here is a solemn party of gentlemen enjoying a social smoke, all seated on the floor of a very fine room indeed. What an important business they make of it! (Page 214.)

Of course the little Tartars (not to speak of the big ones) are fond of stories. All little people enjoy hearing them, but none so much as those who have no books or papers to read. Think if you never saw a story book or magazine, how you would delight in a story teller! Then you can fancy how those little tent-livers crowd around to listen to the tales of the wonderful things that happen to the heroes; the genii, and the magical chairs, and purses, and swords, and other fine things that fill the stories.

Just "make believe" you are in a Tartar tent, and listen to this, a real Tartar story though told in half the words, probably. First I will say that "crump" means crooked, and it is called

"The Three Crump Twin-Brothers.

"There once lived in Damascus an old man who did but just get a poor livelihood by making steel bows, swords, sabres, and knife-blades. Of thirteen children, ten died all in one year, but the three that remained were such odd figures that it was impossible to look at them without laughing.

IN A TARTAR HOUSE.

"They were crooked behind and crooked before, blind of the left eye, lame of the right foot, and so perfectly like one another in face, shape, and clothes, which they always wore the same with one another, that even their father and mother sometimes mistook one for the other.

"Of the three sons the first was named Ibad, the second Syahouk, and the third Babekan, and these three little crump-backed brothers never worked in their shop but they served for laughing stock to all the boys and girls in the town.

"One day as the only son of a rich merchant named Mourad, returned from walking with some of his play-fellows, finding himself more merry than usual, he leaned upon the bulk of the three crumps, and insulted them with so much keenness, that Babekan, who was then at work upon a knife-blade, lost all patience; he ran after those children, and singling out his principal enemy, gave him a cut, but finding that he was pursued by the mob, he ran into the shop and pulled the door after him."

[To make a long story shorter: when the Cadi came, no one could tell which one of the three brothers did the mischief, and as he did not wish to punish the innocent ones, he banished all three of them from Damascus forever. Now go on.]

"Ibad, Syahouk, and Babekan were obliged to comply with the sentence immediately. They departed from the city, and having considered what they should do, Ibad and Syahouk were entirely for keeping together, but Babekan having represented to them, that, let them go where they would, so long as they were together they would always be the jest of the public, but that if they were single, they would each be infinitely less observed; this reason prevailed over the opinion of the two. They parted from each other, and taking each a different road, Babekan came to Bagdad."

[I pass over his adventures for a few years, and begin again after he had become prosperous, the owner of a cutlery shop, and the husband of a woman named Nohoud].

"The correspondence that Babekan had in several towns of the East, came to the ears of his two brothers, who after having lived for almost five years in the utmost poverty, were at last met together at Derbent.

"Here they learnt to their great joy of the prosperity of Babekan, and not doubting but he would assist them in their want, they went together to Bagdad.

"Babekan was prodigiously surprised at the sight of his brothers." He reproached them for breaking their word and coming to make him a jest in Bagdad, and finally he threatened them, and turned them away from Bagdad, with a few pieces of gold to begin again.

When Babekan went home, he told his wife about his brothers, and she tried to persuade him to be more generous with them. At this he got into a fearful rage, and said roughly:

"'I find you will be tempted to entertain them here during the journey I am about to make, but take notice, I would advise you that if you do, it shall cost you your life. I say no more. Look to it that you obey me.'

Nohoud was afraid of her husband, and she said she would execute his orders, and he went away.

But it happened that the two brothers, after going two days' journey from Bagdad, had been obliged to stop. Syahouk had fallen sick, and they were detained till the money was all gone, when they resolved to seek Babekan again. They found that their brother was away on a journey, but his wife was at home, and they went to appeal to her.

"But though Babekan had so strictly commanded her not to

let them into her house, she was touched with their poverty and tears; she let them in and set food before them.

"It was now dark night, and they had scarcely satisfied their first hunger, when somebody rattled at the door. The voice of Babekan was a thunderbolt to his wife and brothers. They turned pale as death, and Nohoud, to conceal them from her husband's fury, hid them in a little cellar, behind five or six tubs of brandy.

"Babekan grew impatient at the door: he knocked louder and louder every moment. At last it was opened, and Babekan, very angry and suspicious, after beating his wife, searched all the house, visiting every hole with the greatest care, but never thought to look behind the brandy tubs.

"He stayed at home till the evening of the next day, when about the hour of prayer he went out. His back was hardly turned when Nohoud ran to the cellar, but was in the utmost surprise at finding Ibad and Syahouk without the least sign of life.

"Her perplexity increased when she considered she had no way of getting rid of the two bodies, but taking her resolution at once, she shut up the shop and ran for a foolish porter, and having told him that a little humpbacked man who came to her shop to buy knives, having died there suddenly, she feared she should be brought into trouble about it, she proffered him four sequins of gold if he would put him in a sack and throw him into the Tygris.

"The porter accepted, and she took him home with her, gave him two sequins by way of earnest, and put only one of the crumps into his sack, and promised to give him the other sequin when she was sure he had performed his commission.

"The porter with the crump upon his shoulder being come to the bridge of Bagdad, opened his sack, shot his load into the river, and running back to Nohoud, 'It is done,' said he, laughing; 'give me the two sequins you promised me.'

"Nohoud then went behind her counter under pretense of fetching him the money, but starting back with a loud cry she pretended to fall into a swoon. The porter was strangely surprised, and after fetching her to herself, he inquired the cause of her fright.

"'Ah!' said the cunning Nohoud, acting her part to a miracle, 'Go in there and you will know the cause.' The porter went in and was struck as mute as a fish, when he perceived the same body which he thought he had thrown into the Tygris.

"'I am sure,' said he, 'I did throw that plaguy crooked rascal into the river; how then could he come hither? There must be witchcraft in it. However,' continued he, 'let us try if he will get out again.'

"Then having put the second crump into the same sack, he carried him to the bridge, and choosing out the deepest part of the Tygris opened his sack, and threw out poor Syahouk.

"He was again returning merrily to Nohoud, not doubting that his burden was gone to the bottom, when, turning the corner of a street, he saw coming toward him a man with a lantern in his hand.

"He was ready to drop dead with fear at the sight of Babekan, who was going home. The porter dogged him a little while, and finding that he took the ready way to the house from which he had fetched the two crumps, he seized him furiously by the collar.

"'Ah, rogue!' cried he, 'you think to make fool of me all

night, do you? You have served me this trick twice already; but if you escape this time, I will be hanged.'

"Then, being a lusty fellow, he threw his sack over Babekan's shoulders, and forcing him into it in spite of his teeth, tied the mouth of it with a strong rope, and running directly to the bridge, flung in poor Babekan, sack and all.

"He walked a pretty while thereabouts, for fear the crump should get out agaim to cheat him of his reward; but, hearing no noise, returned to the cutlaress to demand the other two sequins which she had promised him.

"'Do not fear his coming any more,' said he, the moment he set his foot into the house. 'The wag had a mind to make me his sport forever, I think; he only pretended to be dead that he might make me trot my legs off; but I have done his business for him now so thoroughly, that he will never come to your house any more, I will engage for him.'

"Nohoud was surprised, and on questioning him he told the story, when she cried out that he had drowned her husband, and had the impudence to ask reward." She then declared she would go to the Cadi, and the porter said he would drag her off to the river, too, when the neighbors interfered to protect her.

The porter took to his heels, but soon met three men, each with a load on his head, who forced him to go with them. They entered a dark passage, and at the end of it arrived in a magnificent hall.

"But what was the porter's amazement, when by the light of above forty tapers, with which it was illuminated, he saw the crooked brothers he had thrown into the Tygris. He was seized with such terror that he began to shake all over his body."

[I must tell you in a few words, that the man who had made

him go with them to help carry the loads, was really the Caliph, who was fond of walking the streets of his city at night in disguise, to see for himself how his people liked the government, and how his laws were carried out. On this night he had seen the three bodies hauled up in the net of a fisherman, and had bought his load of him. The terror of the porter betrayed him; and when he was questioned he told the whole story. The Caliph was puzzled; but, seeing signs of life in the bodies, all three were restored to life; indeed, the two brothers had been only overcome with brandy, and Babekan half smothered by the sack.]

"The Caliph having caused the three crumps to be carried into different chambers, had them put to bed and locked up. Then he prepared to divert himself at the expense of the crooked brothers and the cutlar woman, whom he had arrested at break of day.

"To heighten his diversion, the Caliph caused to be made that night two suits of clothes, exactly like that which Babekan wore when he was thrown into the Tygris. He ordered them to be put on to Ibad and Syahouk, whose drunken fit was over, and being all three dressed exactly alike, he placed them behind three different pieces of hanging, in a magnificent hall of the palace, and gave orders that they should be discovered upon his making a certain sign."

Then Nohoud was brought before him as he sat on his throne, and questioned, when she told the truth, and said the brothers were so much alike she thought that even she could not tell them apart if dressed alike. Then the Caliph gave the sign, and the hangings were pulled up, and she saw all three together alive.

THE DESERT.

She was ready to die with fear at the sight, when the Caliph told her she must select her husband. She looked carefully, but could not tell him, and then the Caliph ordered he that was her husband to come forward, when, to her horror, all three came, Ibad and Syahouk to be revenged on Babekan.

It was impossible to tell which was Babekan, for all three declared they were he. After the Caliph had laughed enough at this, he sobered his fun, and told them that perhaps they would not be so anxious to be Babekan if they knew that he was to be bastinadoed.

Then Ibad and Syahouk confessed, and Babekan, with face prostrated to the earth, begged the Caliph to pardon him for cruelty to his brothers, and promised to give them equal shares of his money.

The Caliph was pleased to see him in this spirit, and pardoned him; and now to reward the two brothers for the amusement they had given him, he gave each of them twenty thousand sequins. They each took a wife and settled in Bagdad, "where they traded in fellowship with Babekan, and these three brothers spent the rest of their days in abundance of tranquillity, under the protection of the Sovereign Commander of the Faithful, who was, moreover, so liberal to the porter, that he lived at his ease ever after, without having any occasion for continuing his trade."

This story, which I have been obliged to shorten a little, is taken from a collection of Tales of the East, made more than seventy years ago.

Before we leave the land of the little Tartars, look at a picture of the deserts they have to cross. The sun is just setting, and the travelers must soon pitch their tents for the night.

CHAPTER IX.

THE DYED BABY; THE LITTLE SIAMESE.

NEXT door to the youngster who wears no clothes (at least next door on the map) live the unfortunate little people who are first daubed over with paste, and then smothered.

These are the olive-colored babies of Siam, and life is made hard for them in the cradle I assure you. To begin with, as if nature had not already made than yellow enough, they are well rubbed with a paste made of tumeric and other things with oil. I dare say the Siamese nurse is another one of those conceited people who think they know more than nature herself.

Anyway she does it, and then she puts the greasy, pasty baby in a cradle and covers it up. I should think she'd want to hide such an object as it must be! She covers it up—*head and all!*

You would think it must smother? Well, it sometimes does, bu that doesn't seem to teach them any better. Sometimes indeed the poor little wretch has a muslin cover of a sort of bee-hive shape which would surely be the death of an American baby.

In this secluded way the Siamese youngster spends his first few weeks on earth, every day rubbed with a yellow mixture. Then he is taken up from the cradle, but still kept closely covered till he can walk, when at last comes freedom from wraps.

It is freedom indeed! a few bits of jewelry, a gold chain and a three-inch square of pendant, or similar covering, is considered full dress. The little Siamese who lives through the smothering, and has had his head shaved, excepting a round spot on top, now has his light dress of jewelry put on, and is turned loose to have a good time till he is ten or twelve years old.

Unless indeed he happens to be a royal prince, in which case he is dressed in strange and marvellous array. See him here! Isn't he an object, with a hat like a pagoda, and shoes like a Chinese junk!

Poor little fellow! you would have cause to pity him if this was his every-day dress, but I can assure you that most of his young life is passed as free of clothes as the poorest boy in his country; in this picture he is "dressed up."

In fact that early wrapping up seems to be enough for a whole life, for even the grown-up Siamese wears little covering. One strip of cloth a few yards long, put on in a graceful way, makes the ordinary dress of a man, and with a broad scarf added, which goes over one shoulder, and ties under the other arm, and sometimes a short tunic, is the common dress for women. On page 227 is a picture of the Siamese mother.

Legs and feet go bare, even the king on his throne (at least until lately) merely slips his bare feet into a sort of sandal, and heads are only covered when the sun is hot, and one is obliged to go out.

There's one pleasant thing for the young Siamese—they have plenty of playthings. They do not have to content themselves like the little Turks with rag dolls and a few mean toys. Dolls without end! Poor youngsters' dolls of baked mud, and the dolls of the rich of wood, carved, with clothes on, as in India, or what

DRESSED UP.

is better, made of cloth, something as we make rabbits, or as our good grandmothers used to make dolls for us.

These last, the rag dolls, are dressed like people, and are dearly loved by their little owners. In fact they make much greater ado over their dolls than you do. They have houses for them, which are completely furnished, and children of rich families often have a little garden in which the doll house stands; and then they have feasts (what you would call "having tea" or dinner) and processions, and other fine times.

In a word, the young Siamese girl, exactly as the American one, plays at grown-up life with her dolls. She spends days at a time in her play house, her dolls have their own temple, where they go to church (as we say), they are married and are ill, they die and are buried, just the same as though their little mistress was white and wore dresses and buttoned boots, instead of being yellow, and not wearing much of anything.

You remember I told you in the beginning how much trouble I had in finding out about little folks' life in strange countries. Well, I shouldn't have been able to tell you a thing about the little Siamese, except for one woman. Book after book did I read, of travels in Siam, and page after page of history, and talk about their government, and their temples, and their country, but not a word about anybody less than five feet high. You'd have thought the babies were *all* smothered in those dreadful cradles.

But happily an English woman—Mrs. Leonowens—has spent several years in the family of the king of Siam, as governess; better still, she has written some books for us; and best of all, she has kindly told for your benefit other things about child life. You have her to thank for all I am able to tell you about these queer little people.

SIAMESE MOTHERS.

The young Siamese that she tells us the most about are of the royal family of course, and I must tell you where they lived. Their home is in the most curious city in the world, a city of women and children alone. It is in the middle of the city of Bangkok, has high walls all around it, and a population of nine thousand people, yet not a man lives in it.

In this strange place, called city of Nang Harm (or veiled women), there are shops and markets, temples and theatres; there are streets and avenues, little parks and lakes, trees and flower gardens; there is a hall of justice, with its judges and executioners, and its dungeons attached; there are police, guards, and soldiers, all, from first to last, women. Look at one of the women soldiers.

That is not all. This city is as complete as any, it needs no help from outside; besides shops for the sale of goods, it has all sorts of mechanics, carpenters, jewelers, and others, and all women.

One man alone in all Siam can enter when he likes, the king. It is the home of his family, and the family of the king before him. You know, perhaps, that in Siam a man may have several wives, and a king as many as he pleases. Each wife has her own children and slaves, and therefore a city is needed to give room for all.

On one occasion a procession of men is admitted; they are priests, and since the Siamese believe that giving to the priests is necessary to religion, it would be cruel to deprive the women of Nang Harm of the chance of being charitable. Therefore a guard is appointed, of the women soldiers, to escort the priests through one of the principal streets, from one gate straight across to another. They hold out their bowls as they go, and

A GIRL SOLDIER.

the women fill them with food. Excepting the king, and these priests in procession every morning, no man ever sets his foot in the city.

Should you like to see the head of this strange city? Here he is.

This is the picture of a king now dead, with his queen. The pupil of the English lady that I spoke of is now king of Siam, and he dresses more as we do.

In this city of veiled women lived the English governess' little pupils. You probably fancy that life in a palace must be delightful, but it is far from that to the princes of Siam. A free, careless, happy life like yours they know nothing of; life is stern and hard, even in the cradle.

The first lesson the poor little things are taught is to be silent, and the next to be suspicious, and afraid of everybody. They are little men and women before they are out of the nursery.

This seems very sad; let us turn to a pleasanter picture. These little people are well supplied with playthings. They have doll houses of all sorts, from the bamboo hut, which floats on the river, in which many people of Siam live, as you see on page 232, to the king's palace itself. Each house has its complete furniture, and set of dolls in proper dress. They have also doll temples, with doll priests, ships with doll sailors, and so on.

Then they have china toy dishes, ivory furniture, and hundreds of other toys. As I told you above, Siamese girls make more of their dolls than you do; they have elaborate dinners of several courses, they perform plays, they have various ceremonies, as in real Siamese life.

But even their doll life the princesses can't enjoy as you do. Though they are deeply interested in everything, they do not

KING AND QUEEN.

handle the dolls themselves; they look on while the slaves do the playing for them! Think of having slaves to play for you! Poor children!

They have other amusements; there are fish and birds to feed, there are swings and bathing places to enjoy, there are back-

A FLOATING HOME.

gammon and chess, and Chinese cards; there is singing to be heard, and dancing to be seen; there are theatrical performances, where the actors are the funniest creatures you ever saw.

See them here! Look at the moustache on the actor on the right, and the head dresses of the others. See the bare feet, and the wings on one, and above all, look at the finger-nails of the middle one. You see they are several inches long. These may be false ones, but nails are really grown as long as these, and it's a queer idea of ornament, isn't it?

Besides these there are stories to be listened to (and slaves to tell them), and above all there are flowers. Flowers are a great

ACTORS.

source of pleasure in the City of Nang Harm. The children make garlands of them to wear around the waist, or on the head, or to hang on the arm; and a flower behind the ear is like a buttonhole bouquet to us.

One flower in particular, which is so fragrant, that one blossom will fill a room with odor, is the champa, of a yellow color, and is almost always worn behind the ear of a child.

They have shuttlecock, which they play with the foot; they have quoits and wrestling, and they have puppet-shows of many kinds.

Another amusement which they particularly like, is watching the feats of gymnasts. This picture of one of these performances, which was seen and described by Mrs. Feudge in *St. Nicholas*, was drawn by a Siamese artist, and he did not show how high the poles really were. The men, you see, are on a swing, and as they swing back and forth, each man has one chance to seize in his mouth a purse full of gold, which is forty feet from the ground. If he gets it, it is his to keep, and he goes down from the swing by a rope-ladder; but if he does not, he is not only laughed at, but he is obliged to let go of the ropes, sieze the pole on which the purse hangs, and slide down to the ground.

But above all pleasures they have the kite! This, which is not a specially favorite plaything with us, is the best loved sport over nearly all Asia. In India, as I told you, they are usually square, in Siam they are of different shapes, butterflies, birds, and others, and they are flown by men, women, and children.

Their going to church is odd to us. The temple has no seats, but the whole floor (at least of the princesses temple) is of polished brass. On this the people seat themselves in little circles all over the floor, each person having standing before her a vase of flowers and a lighted taper, and all are dressed in white. It must be a pretty sight.

The priest wears a robe of yellow, with a fan held before his face. From behind the fan he chants a prayer, and the groups

WILL HE GET IT?

on the floor raise themselves to their knees, and bow their heads to the floor, in response to the prayer. Then they sit still and listen to a little sermon, and that is all. There is no singing, and no standing up.

But their schools, especially the girls' schools, would be funny to see. Boys are taught to read and write and cypher, but girls are taught by rote. This is not only in the woman's city, but in all well-to-do families in Siam. In these droll school-rooms no books are used. There may be a map of the world on the wall which would make you laugh. It represents Siam as a great country in the middle of the world, Burmah a very small patch on the north, and all the rest sea.

When the English governess showed them a globe and large map of the world, the children were very much interested, and crowded around asking questions as fast as a crowd of you, perhaps. At first they were a little disappointed to see their dear Siam, which they had thought the very centre of everything, as a little speck of earth on one side, but they soon consoled themselves when they found out that England, which makes so much noise in the world, is not even so large.

They were very anxious to know about the sun, moon, and stars; not however because they were interested in astronomy, but because they supposed them to be the homes of hobgoblins, demons, and other not very agreeable neighbors. One little scholar really refused to believe that the lovely moon is a stupid ball of earth, but insisted that she is a beautiful woman, daughter of a great king, and head wife of the sun.

But I must tell you how the girls are taught; manners of course, especially to carry the left arm so that the elbow sticks out forward, which is thought to be very elegant; and all the

CALLING ON A KING.

other little points of polite etiquette which are important in so ceremonious a part of the world as this, where no one approaches the king except crawling on hands and knees, on the ground, as you see in this picture of a king of a neighboring state, receiving a French traveler. (See page 237.)

The king is a Laotian, and the attitude of his people, creeping like babies, is the same that the Siamese king of that time required.

[I must remind you again that I am trying to picture the lives of these little foreigners to you, as they were before the English and other European people had made changes in their native ways. It is the *native* Siamese I want to show you, not the English taught Siamese.]

Let us go back to the girls' school. The scholars are placed in a row, with certain attendant officers, armed with rattans, whose business it is to see that no girl shirks her lesson. They are to learn singing, poems to repeat, dancing or gymnastics, and not a book to be seen, unless possibly the teacher has one. The teacher begins. Suppose it is a song, she sings the first line (or part of a line), the head pupil sings it after her, then the next one sings it, and so on to the end of the row. Then they sing it all together. When they all know that line, they go on to the next, till they can sing the whole air.

In this way they learn everything, simply "by heart," and the one who is most like a parrot to remember words, is the best scholar. A dancing class of this sort must be amusing to see, or one in gymnastics. They learn a great deal, the poor youngsters, often as many as a hundred songs and poems, which they sing and repeat the rest of their lives. No papers and magazines for the little Siamese girl, no St. Nicholas, no new

SOLEMN HAIR CUTTING.

books, nothing but those old, old stories, and songs. How dreadful!

There is one point they are careful about, they never learn an even number of stories or songs; it must be ninety-nine or a hundred and one, never ninety-eight or a hundred. They are very superstitious about this dislike for even numbers, and carry it so far that they never have even numbers of windows or doors nor of steps in a flight of stairs.

But little people grow up fast in these warm countries, and while you are still pegging away at arithmetic, grammar, and other charming sciences, the young Siamese come of age. This is a great time in their life, as of course it is in yours, but they show it in a different way. The girls do not simply put on long dresses, and the boys grow a moustache; they both *have their hair cut!*

The hair is a serious matter I can tell you. In the first place they shave it all off in babyhood, as I told you, excepting a round spot on top of the head. This grows and is taken care of, "done up" in a coil, dressed with flowers, and held in place by large pins of gold and jewels, or of porcupine quills among the poor. When a child is old enough to put away childish things and take its place as a man, great ceremonies take place with those who can afford it, and, as I said above, the hair is cut.

A poor man's child is taken to a temple, and the priests go through some religious ceremony, and remove the hair; but a rich man's child, and above all a royal youth, has great doings over this little matter. An artificial hill or mountain is built, and adorned with trees and animals, gilding and various gorgeous decorations, and having a path leading to the top.

LADIES AT DINNER.

In the midst of feasting, and processions, and great entertainments, such as dramas with thousands of actors which last several days, the child is led up this hill, with some one walking before him shaking a rattle to imply that he is still in infancy, and accompanied by those who are to take place in the ceremony. At the top, in a place prepared, the religious ceremonies are performed, and the hair is cut. The proud young prince or princess, who went up an infant with a rattle box before him (or her) marches down a man, or woman.

On page 239 is a youth going through this ceremony. You see the two priests with their bowls before them, and the young fellow himself on his knees.

Henceforth the hair on this round place will be kept cut rather short, and standing straight up like a hair brush, while all the rest of the head is clean shaven. And now, too, the time draws near when the young people must marry. Though not so young as in India, girls of fourteen are considered of a proper age, and sixteen is not too young for a boy.

You see the picture of ladies at dinner; they eat from the same dish, and with the fingers as you see. The poorer people live principally on rice, but the rich eat nearly everything.

There are some very queer houses in Siam, especially in Bangkok. They are floating houses, built on bamboo rafts, and held together by chains. There are shops and markets, and in fact they form a part of the city by themselves. You had a picture of these on page 232.

They go about, of course, in boats, and have their street peddlers as we do, shouting their wares at the top of their voices, and each in his own boat.

The canoes, in which these boat people get about, are man-

ENTRANCE TO PALACE.

aged very easily by the very babies of a few years old. These youngsters spend half their time in the water, swim and dive, and enjoy it as much as so many ducks.

The finest houses in Siam are, of course, those belonging to the king; and to show you what sort of building these people think the finest, here is the picture of one.

ON THE RIVER.

See the grim-looking giants with their great clubs, to guard the door, and scare away unwelcome visitors. You can see by the man between them how tall they are.

But the ordinary homes of the little Siamese are built of bamboo, one story high, and thatched with palm leaves, as you see in this one, on the banks of the river Menam, which is also built on poles, to be out of water in case the river rises.

In the same picture you can see another sort of boat, with queer sails.

Inside, the houses are almost alike. The home of the rich youngsters has fine mats on the floor, and the walls hung with white muslin, but not much furniture except a low couch covered with mats, on which they sit by day, and sleep at night, as

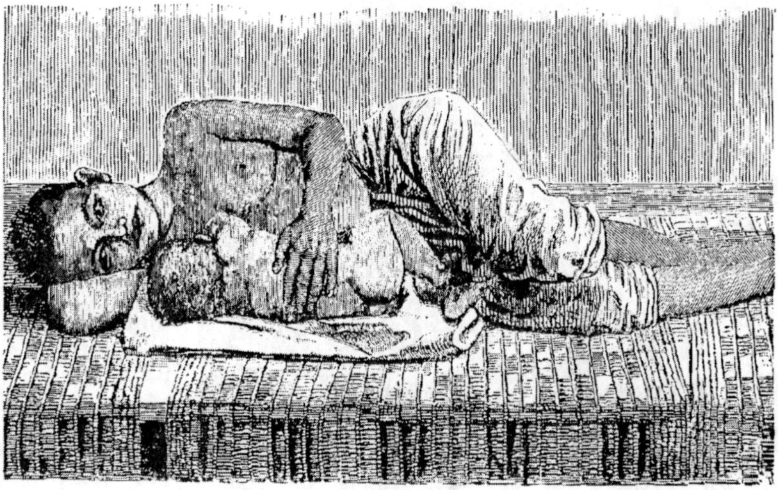

BABY AND NURSE.

you see this nurse is doing with a little fellow, who has, happily, got past the smothering process of his early baby days.

Cabinets, copper, and earthen vessels, and china, are pretty much all there is besides, and in the home of the poor little people, there is of course still less.

Perhaps a stranger house than the Siamese proper, is found close by, among the Laotians, where you go up by means of a ladder, and when you don't care for visitors you simply draw it up after you.

In this next picture you can see how the house is built, of bamboo bound together, and not nailed as we should do, and also how look the mothers who live there. No shaved heads here, you see! But what queer ways to "do up" the hair! one looks like a bird perched on the head. And what fine, beautiful baskets they carry!

HOME OF THE LITTLE LAOTIAN.

The funniest thing about these people, at least that a traveler can see, is the sort of saddles they make for their elephants. On page 249 you see a caravan of these huge animals crossing a river. It shows how they slide down a steep hill, and it also shows a baby elephant.

LAOTIAN MOTHERS.

Now this baby may be very interesting to see; most babies are, but it's a great nuisance on a march, I can tell you. The reason is, that it is, like other young things, always getting into trouble of some sort, and the moment it cries out, every old elephant of the troop will run to help it. If it happens to fall into a ravine, down will go every big elephant pell-mell after the careless baby, and that you see is not very pleasant for the riders, perched up in these queer coops on their backs.

QUEER SADDLES

Other strange little people in the same part of the world are the Cambodians, who live in a house like that on page 250, get about on water in the boat before the house, and on land ride in a cart like that on page 251, which is drawn by two oxen.

The mamma of these little people holds up her great coil of hair with an arrow, and wears more clothes than the Siamese mother.

CAMBODIAN MOTHER

In fact, we're getting pretty near to China, as you will see if you look on a map of Asia, and the people begin to look a little Chinese.

HOME OF THE LITTLE CAMBODIAN.

Great changes have taken place in Siam since the little prince whom Mrs. Leonowens taught, has become a man, and is king; and no doubt in time the lives of the children will be very different.

But, though it is pleasant to see people improve, it will always be interesting to know how they lived when they worked out their own ways, and did not copy anybody.

HIS CARRIAGE.

Of course you would like to hear a real Siamese story; well, here's one that will show you exactly how these queer people tell their stories. It is taken from Bowring's Siam, and begins thus:

"Now I am about to republish a story. At the time when the vacuum was in existence, and all things were in the most profound silence, long, long ago, in olden time, there was a kingdom called Chambank. The king bore the name Chambank Rachareteret, and his queen was the Lady Chantahtawee. She was both amiable and dutiful, and a thousand times fair and slender; her countenance was very handsome, her deportment elegant, and she was quite superior to all her maids of honor.

"Now I would speak in praise of the kingdom. The whole surface was covered with an immense population, who lived extremely contented, and filled with happiness; the symmetry of their bodies adorned the kingdom—"

Dear me! how many words! let us skip a little. I will quote farther on about the queen's baby.

"Now, my readers, I must speak about the beauty of this exalted child, because it was of royal extraction and parentage. When it was born it was wonderful! There was a wonder; the stars sparkled, shone, and glistened with immense beauty, and in the universe, the angels gathering in crowds pronounced a blessing, and strewed flowers, the fragrance of which penetrated every corner."

This is a little too Siamese in style. I think you will like better one that Mrs. Leonowens has told in her "Romance of the Harem." It is a genuine Siamese story, with some of the extra words left out, and explains, in one way, the origin of gold and silver mines. I must add that many people believe it to be true.

"A SIAMESE LEGEND.

"Vela Chow, or the Beautiful Dawn, was the only daughter of a very powerful king of Ayudia. She was so wondrously beautiful that the old Brahmins and astrologers who foretold her birth, named her before she was born, the Beautiful Dawn, as the only appropriate name for her.

"Now it happened that at this time there was no moon to illuminate the fair earth, but the golden sun and the green earth enjoyed a much closer, and more intimate friendship than they now do, and old age, and sickness, and death were unknown to the blessed and undying people of Ayudia.

"But as the mighty king, Somdetch P'hra Batt, the Duke of the Golden Foot, had reigned nearly thirty-five hundred years without ceasing, he became weary of the cares of state, and therefore abdicated in favor of his young son P'hra Batt Bandethano, a vigorous youth, of not more than five hundred years of age, who was even from his childhood an especial favorite of the ruby-faced and warm-hearted monarch, P'hra Athiett, that is, the sun.

"In the course of time the friendship between these two, sovereigns of the earth and sky, ripened to such a degree of perfection, that the latter was loath to withdraw his bright beaming face from his young friend's kingdom, even to seek his couch for a little rest at night, as had been his custom from time immemorial. Thus he beamed forth both night and day in saffron hues on the fair mountains and lovely valleys of the invincible city of Ayudia, and the land flourished in luxuriance and beauty, the fruits and flowers rivalled those that grew and blossomed in Indra's own garden, and countless birds of marvelous plumage winged their flight from distant worlds, to build their nests and warble their melodies among the proud forests of that favored land.

"As for the men of this region, they were tall and stately, and of golden mien, like the laughter-loving gandharwas of Indra's paradise; and the women were gloriously beautiful, fair as silvery clouds, with eyes of wondrous hue.

"Away flew the golden days and nights, and round and round rushed the radiant chariot wheels of P'hra Athiett, and thousands and thousands of years sped away, but he never relaxed the speed of his swift coursers, nor drew in his rainbow-tinted reins, nor turned away even for an instant his glowing eyes from this favored kingdom.

"Now things having gone on in this way for several thousands of years, yet no sweet slumber had ever closed the god-like eyes of P'hra Athiett, and all the lovely Dowastras, or stars, finding themselves totally eclipsed, their brilliancy and beauty marred by this unceasing sleeplessness on the part of their sovereign, formed the wicked and cruel design of revolting against him, and of taking possession, by some means or other, of his golden car.

"Accordingly, instead of going to sleep as had been their practice during the day, they all plotted together to hide themselves behind the many-tinted curtain of their monarch's chariot and to watch his movements, in order to discover the cause of the singular attraction that drew him forever toward the earth, while he left his own vaulted and ethereal hemisphere to the tender mercies of stray suns, or wandering comets.

"Having ratified by many a vow their wicked compact, the treacherous Dowastras, instead of going to bed like the dutiful children of a kind and beneficient ruler, only pretended to sleep, but all the while kept opening and shutting, and blinking their bright little eyes, winking at one another, and peering behind the golden curtains of the royal chariot at their unconscious master, who, fully believing that all his subjects were sound asleep, grew brighter and brighter, while over his round, genial face there beamed forth a smile of ineffable radiance, as he approached the earth.

"At this very moment the rebellious Dowastras, wondering at the blissful face of their monarch, peered out from behind the rainbow-hued drapery of the celestial chariot and turned their penetrating eyes toward the earth, when to their astonishment they beheld the face of Vela Chow, who was lulling her wearied father to rest with the music of her sweet voice.

"'Ah ha!' laughed the wicked Dowastras, 'now we have found out the secret!'

"As soon as she had soothed her father to sleep, the lovely Vela Chow, all unconscious of what was happening around her, sauntered forth among the unfrequented woods and dells, making the voiceless hills and rocks re-echo her notes in melodious sounds."

[I omit a long account of her wanderings.]

"At last she sat herself down in the deep solitude to rest, and as she listened to the gentle zephyrs that fanned her yellow tresses, ... it chanced that a gorgeous butterfly, more glorious than any that she had ever before seen, alighted on a neighboring flower. Up sprang Vela Chow, and away she flew after it, from flower to flower, from shrub to tree, till at last the tantalizing butterfly flew so high in the air, that the eager damsel could do no more than raise her fair face and sparkling eyes to follow its airy flight through the bright sky.

"Just at this moment P'hra Athiett's golden chariot was coming over the hill, and he smiled a smile of such ineffable delight when he caught sight of her, that he dazzled the eyes of the poor little maiden; and as she could no longer see the beautiful butterfly, she was obliged to relinquish all idea of capturing it.

"So she retraced her disconsolate steps to her lonely mountain stream, and plunged into its waters in the hope of finding therein refreshment and forgetfulness of her cruel disappointment. But P'hra Athiett was not to be thus baffled; so he noiselessly climbed higher and higher, and came nearer and nearer, and smiled so much more warmly than ever, that he once more quite overpowered the weary maiden, who suddenly vanished from his sight, sought refuge in her favorite mountain cavern, and there fell sound asleep.

"For a moment poor P'hra Athiett was disconcerted, and a great pain, like a dark, heavy cloud, shot up from his breast, and overspread his bright, happy face, and he knew not what to do; but the next he broke forth into a more joyous smile than ever, for he was just as foolish as he was old, and had been on the lookout all these thousands of years, hoping to catch a glimpse of this incomparable maiden, and now he could not make up his mind to perform his journey without one more look at her sweet, pure face."

So (to cut a long story a little short), he turned around and drove down the mountain side to her cavern, went in, and smiled on her till she awoke. But, while they were conversing (to resume), "the wicked Dowastras, in all haste, rushed to the mountain side, drove off the golden chariot, and unharnessed the swift-winged coursers. Having thus cut off his retreat, they raised a shout of triumph, deposed their monarch, and established a republic among themselves, permitting neither stray suns nor wandering comets to have anything to do with their government.

"Poor P'hra Athiett, who had persuaded the sweet Vela Chow to be his bride, found now, to his consternation and grief, that his golden chariot had vanished. He bowed his head, and his great joyous face became suddenly overcast, all its light and glory departed, while large tears like mountain torrents rolled from his god-like eyes, and streamed upon the earth, and were then and there transformed into nuggets of the purest gold.

"Then the mountains, pitying his sufferings, opened their hearts, and revealed to him a secret passage, by which he might regain his heavenly abode.

P'hra Athiett bade adieu to Vela Chow, and started off, promising to return, tears falling all the way. As for Vela Chow, she followed on after him, shedding rivers of tears, which turned into veins of purest silver.

"Thus the grief of these two god-like hearts served to enrich the country with endless wealth.

After twelve hours the wicked Dowastras repented, and made a new compact with P'hra Athiett. In this they agreed, "that for a fortnight in every month he should pick up his beautiful bride at the mouth of the cavern, and take her with him to his celestial home, but that for the rest of the month she should unveil her matchless face, and reveal her exquisite beauty to the Dowastras, and rule over them in the sky, for they all loved her;" and they changed her name to Rupea Chandra, the Silver Moon.

"But even to this day, when Vela Chow is presiding in splendor over the jealous Dowastras, P'hra Athiett is foolish enough at times to attempt to kiss her, when all the Siamese, fearing lest he should again be dethroned, turn out *en masse*, and shout, and beat drums, and fire cannons, to warn him of the impropriety of his proceedings, which in the space of two or three hours (this being the time, it is said, that sound takes to get to the

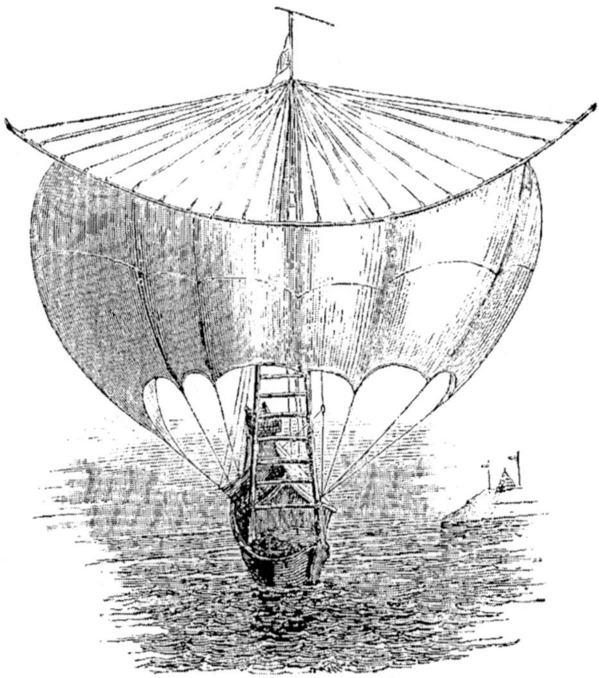

THE ODDEST YET.

moon), generally produces the desired effect of recalling the monarch to himself. Thus are gold and silver mines, and lunar and solar eclipses accounted for, and annual pilgrimages are still made to the cavern where Vela Çhow plighted her troth to P'hra Athiett."

BURMAN ACTOR.

You have seen some strange looking boats, but this is perhaps the strangest of all. It is used by the people of Burmah, another neighbor to Siam, where the little people learn to smoke cigars before they can walk. Boys, and girls too, smoke from morning till night.

Even in school the smoking goes on, and the little scholar only lays it aside while he recites his lesson, which he bawls at the top of his voice, like other little Asiatics.

MUSICIAN.

I want to show you an actor of Burmah, because it is curious to see how different are people who live side by side. Look at her on page 259. How unlike the Siamese!

She is performing, you see, and she has no stage, and no roof over her. It is in the open air, and anybody can hear that can get near enough.

Look at the curious kind of a drum the man is playing behind her. Here is a better picture of it, and of another Burman instrument, which you might mistake for a big tub, or some sort of a cage.

This is the queer country, where one of your plays (you boys), the one you call the "tug of war," is a religious ceremony. They perform it when the country needs rain, and it is curious to see.

The rope, or what takes the place of your rope, is made of long canes twisted together, with sticks thrust through to take hold of. The boys and men of one town take hold one side, and those of another town take the other side, and then both pull as hard as they can.

ANOTHER.

Each side has one of the curious instruments like the pictures, and its own priest to encourage to hard work.

This tug of war, performed in a solemn manner, with music and priests, is seriously thought to bring rain. And it doesn't matter which side beats either, for they all want the rain.

You think it is odd that your play begins as a religious ceremony. So it is; but dancing too was a part of religion, and is even now, in some places.

These youngsters of Burmah, who smoke while still in arms, are the babies which you see resting by the roadside in their queer baby carriages, in the first chapter.

CHAPTER X.

BABIES UNDER THE SNOW; LITTLE SIBERIANS.

AWAY up there in the snow, near the north pole, where winter is one long, long night, and summer almost like one long day, are other queer little people.

There is one, whose cradle is a wall-pocket; truly, a pocket of fur, on the skin walls of his father's tent. He is, I'm sure, safe, and out of the way in that crowded little tent, and above all, he is warm, and to be warm is almost the one object of life in that part of the world.

When this pocketed youngster is big enough to roll around, he is tied up in a lot of furs till he looks like a big bundle, and then he can live on the floor with his elders. Then he can eat fat meat, learn to drive and take care of reindeer, and grow up into a gloomy, silent man, or, if the baby happens to be a girl, she will learn to dress furs, to sew, and to keep house like her mother.

These little people are Samoides, and we should know more about their ways if it were not so dreadfully cold up there that no one can bear to stay who knows enough to get away.

On page 264 is a picture of the home they live in. Dreary looking place, isn't it? It is livelier than usual, too, just now, for a ship is coming near, and everybody, little and big, is out to see the wonder.

HOME OF YAKOUTE YOUNGSTERS.

In this dismal part of the world lives also this queer baby, whose dress is so odd, and who is so interested in the dead animal her father has brought home, that she doesn't turn around and show us her face. At the back of the picture you see her home, a low hut. This youngster is a Mandchouse. I wonder if you can find her home on the map!

HOME OF SAMOIDES LITTLE PEOPLE.

Not far from these people are other strange houses and little folk. (See page 263.) The dress of the children is not so very odd; but look at the grown-ups and their tent houses.

And then look at a mamma of these children. No doubt she is very elegant, and in the height of fashion, with her cheeks and chin decorated, her funny hat like a pair of cow's horns, and the dangling ball fringe to her dress. Page 267.

You see she's out hunting, for she has her bows and arrows. If she wished to ride she would take a pair of reindeer, and a

MANDCHOUSE BABY.

sledge, or what might be called a skeleton sleigh, like this which the father of this queer family is about to use.

I have shown you the dancers and actors of several races in

Asia: look at page 269! Isn't it the strangest yet? You see the ball fringe is very popular. On the ground you can see a mask, which, probably, the dancer has thrown off in her excitement. These are the Yakoutes.

Now here's a sensible dress for the terrible climate of northern Siberia, where the babies I have been telling about all live. See it on page 268.

ON A JOURNEY.

It is not a bear, as you might suppose, which the lady is so carefully directing on his way. It is her son, in his winter dress of fur, which comes up over his head, and covers his face like a mask, having holes for eyes, and nose, and mouth. I don't see how that youngster can be cold.

YAKOUTE MAMMA.

But see him in his summer dress on page 270, with his cap like a policeman's cap, his full gathered trowsers and turned-up shoes. In summer you see mamma is quite fine in dress, and their home is in a comfortable house. They are people of Bere-

BEAR OR BOY?

zov, and this is their traveling carriage on page 272. No two of the people who drive reindeer, harness them up in the same way.

I'm afraid you don't realize how cold it is up in this country. Milk is carried about in bricks, with a string frozen in. This

A QUEER DANCE.

string may be fastened to one's girdle, and the milk allowed to dangle there till wanted to drink, or to eat, wouldn't you say?

Soup is always carried in blocks, and a favorite meat for

IN SUMMER.

travelers is like marbles. A traveler takes a bag of these with him, and when he wishes to eat he thaws them out in hot water.

Apples in this freezing place grow about as big as whortle-

HOW PLANTS GROW.

berries, with seeds the size of a small pin-head. The little folks don't eat them as you do apples; they are pickled to eat with meat.

In this charming place the children sit on top of the stove!

A SLEIGH RIDE.

But then the stove is not like ours, it is a brick affair, as you see in this picture, where the baby is enjoying the warmth. This

Siberian cradle you see is something like that of the Hindu baby, so far away to the south.

Storms in Siberia are fearful; the wind is so strong that it blows people away, and they are lost in going a few steps, and

SIBERIAN CRADLE.

so cold that they are often frozen solid while walking, so solid and so suddenly, that they are left standing like statues of ice. Hailstones fall as large as millstones, and snowstorms are blinding, like that on page 275.

But in spite of the cold, some plants grow to an enormous size. Fennel, which with us is low enough for the littlest of you to pick, grows to be twelve feet high, with bunches of blossoms, and seeds a foot and a half across, as in the picture on page 271.

If there was a man in the picture he would not reach more than half way up these plants.

Bears are very fond of this fennel, and bears are plenty in Siberia. They come down from the mountains to seek the green food, and then the Siberian boy's papa goes out to hunt them. Here he is on page 276, after a mother bear with two cubs. The old lady looks as though she meant to make it rather lively for the brave man who dares to attack her at such close quarters.

Strange to say, one of the most famous bear hunters of Siberia a few years ago was a young girl. Her brothers were hunters, and hearing them talk she made up her mind to try for herself. She stole off alone to hunt her first bear, and astonished the family by bringing home a skin. After that she went whenever she chose, and became famous all through Siberia, as Mr. Atkinson tells us in his interesting book.

Her name is Anna Petrovnaia, and she no doubt lived in a bare looking house like that on page 277, where the family are at their prayers before an image.

Summer is not so dreadful as winter, of course, but even then traveling is not very charming, with the wild horses three abreast in Russian fashion Here is a traveler who barely escaped with his life. (See page 278.)

The little people of Siberia have no doubt plays and play-things of some sort, but the only game I can find out about is one of the girls' plays. It is what we call a "Teeter," a plank put across a support on which two or more can go up and down.

OUT IN THE STORM.

The Siberian teeter rests on a support only a few inches from the ground, and a girl stands on each end. When one girl goes up, she is thrown into the air, then she comes down hard, and jounces the other up a little higher, and so they go on, fifteen

LOOK OUT FOR YOURSELF.

or twenty minutes at a time, till they are thrown three or four feet straight up every time. They must have some bad falls before they get expert at this.

Do you want to see the father and mother of these unfortunate little Siberians? Look on page 279.

HOME OF SIBERIAN LITTLE FOLK.

In this cold country, too, are the little folk of Lapland; black eyed, flat-faced creatures, whose cradle is shaped like a shoe, covered with fur and stuffed with moss, carried on mamma's back when she goes out, and sometimes buried in the snow, with a dog to guard when she goes in to church.

JUST A MISS.

This seems dreadful, to be sure, but we've seen so many queer things about babies in far-away Asia, that nothing can surprise us now, however odd.

The little Lapps live all huddled up "higglety-pigglety" with the grown-ups in a skin tent, sometimes only six feet in diameter, or not so large as a small bath-room in a city house. Think of a whole family living in such a place!

And they receive guests, too, even in so small a house. The family will all crowd together on one side and leave the other for a stranger, with the fire in the middle. Yet, after all, a Lapp youngster has a pretty good time. His cradle, if queer, is comfortable. It is stuffed with moss to make it soft, and baby is

FATHER AND MOTHER.

wrapped in a sheet, and fastened in by cords laced across the opening. Here he sleeps day and night, only coming out for his daily bath, till he is old enough to walk.

As soon as a Lapp baby is born, a reindeer is given to him, to begin a little fortune for him when grown up. Not only that deer but all its young, and as they grow up all their young deer belong to the child, so that when he is of age he has quite a little herd of his own.

The play of the little Lapp is a good deal like work, for he has a hard life before him. He must learn to be expert on snow-shoes, for on them he gets about in winter. He practices on them till he can not only walk and run, go up and go down, but can jump several feet down and not fall, and if you don't think that's hard to do, suppose you try it some time.

Boys and girls, like their fathers and mothers, dress almost exactly alike in Lapland, and they go to school if they live in a village, where they sit on the floor and study all together.

If they live far from each other, a wandering teacher comes around from house to house and teaches the youngsters, for all Lapp children must learn to read at least.

Little Lapps, like the Siberian boy in the picture you saw, have masks of fur for cold, windy weather, and they have also big caps with several inches of down in the top, to keep their heads warm. Their boots and mittens are big, and stuffed with dry grass, and they sleep in long fur gowns like bags, dressed in all their day clothes.

CHAPTER XI.

MORE HALF-FROZEN BABIES; THE LITTLE ESKIMO.

ABOVE all, up there in the snow, lives the Eskimo little man, whom we know more about than any of the rest of these half-frozen little folk, and who is for that reason, perhaps, the most interesting of all.

This is no screaming or howling baby, who keeps a nurse busy all day attending to his wants, and half the house awake all night for the same purpose. Far from it; the Eskimo baby is a model. He very rarely cries, and never gets cross. Here he is with the rest of the family, on the next page.

To be sure he hasn't much to trouble him, no clothes to pinch him, and always warm in the soft fur nest where his baby days are spent. The nest is mamma's hood, and there, cuddled down close to her warm neck, the little fellow has no reason to be anything but very, very good.

A little trouble comes to babies among one tribe of Eskimos, but they're so young they know nothing about it. They have their heads squeezed. You remember we have found a good many nations who think nature doesn't know how to fashion a baby, and so they complete the job themselves. Well; the Eskimos belong to that sort of people. They want baby's head a certain shape, so they take it in their hands and—squeeze it into the fashionable shape! Then, lest it should go back, they put on a little skin cap, which is tight, and holds the poor little head as they wish it to be. This cap is worn for a year.

CRADLE AND BABY AND ALL.

The youngster and his mother have a bran new house for themselvės, and when the little Eskimo is two weeks old, his mother goes out to make calls. She throws away her old clothes, and calls at every house or *igloo* in the settlement.

Till it is three years old the little one has no clothes, but rolls around on the beds or the floor in the house, and always goes out in the warm nest I told you about. If he happens to be naughty, which is a rare thing, he is quickly taught to behave, by exposing him to the enemy of his life, the thing he has to fight as long as he lives, the cold. In one place the naughty Eskimo child is held in the sea till it stops crying. No matter how cold it may be, even in the middle of winter, the Alaska Eskimo is thus trained. Those who are not killed by this curious sea bathing, get very tough, and are able to go bare footed even in winter.

In another place, to teach the unruly youngster to behave, he is tossed out into the snow and cold, naked, you remember. This very soon cures him of any naughtiness.

If the poor young one lives through these performances, and gets to be three years old, he is thought big enough to be dressed. So a suit is prepared, which is exactly like his father's, for the boy, and like the mother's for a girl. There's not much difference in the suits, probably you could not tell boys from girls in the Eskimo dress. The girls' coats or frocks, or whatever one might call the dress (they call it *parky*), is a little longer than the boys', and has a bigger hood. Here is a boy on the next page, who looks comfortable, doesn't he?

But let me tell you what the dress is. It is a sort of loose jacket, buttoned at the waist, and made of fur, of course; below this is worn a pair of fur trowsers, and then boots. The woman's boots are curious affairs, made to hold lots of things besides her feet. In fact, they look more like big bags than like boots, and have to be held up by a broad strap which is fastened to her girdle.

Maybe you girls think there isn't much chance for trimming on the Eskimo girls' dress, but if you do you're greatly mistaken. No flowers to be sure, no ruffles or puffs, no ribbons or laces; but other things she likes better. To begin with, she can have a sort of breast-plate, a *plastron* (to be elegant) of bead work, and then fringes of various kinds, from all parts of her dress. One very grand dress in Eskimo land is described by a traveler as nearly covered with ornaments. Listen! across the neck in front was a bead of fringe of several colors; hanging from the pointed flap of the dress in front was a fringe made of the bowls of britannia tea-spoons, which must certainly have been gorgeous.

IN FULL DRESS.

But the back was a study. The long piece hanging down from the jacket had a fringe made of common lead shot, drawn out long, and through the middle a double row of copper cents, with, at their head, a big brass gong out of an old clock! There! wasn't that gown trimmed?

Life is not all work with the little people, they have toys in plenty. The girls have dolls; some little ones carved from ivory not more than an inch long, and others of ivory or wood sometimes more than a foot tall, and dressed from top to toe in the most stylish Eskimo dress. These large ones have eyes made of bits of pearly shells, and noses, too, which gives them a droll expression.

The black-eyed mistresses of these dolls love them quite as much as you do yours, and play with them too. For them they build the tiny snow-hut, and beg of mamma a bit of wick for a lamp lest dolly should freeze; in their small hoods go the tiny ivory babies an inch long, while the doll itself is carried in the hood of its little mistress.

The boys have toy sledges and boats, and even imitations of the white man's ship, with rigging of sinews or the fine roots of a certain grass. They have, too, tiny spears, bows and arrows, lances, and so forth, and both have animals of all the kinds known to Eskimos, bears, seals, whales, dogs, and others. They play at their fathers' life also, they hunt the ivory seal, shoot the toy bears, draw the little sledges.

But little people soon learn to help father and mother in the hard work of life. Boys get expert in killing birds on the wing, and when only eight or nine years old, begin to go with their fathers to hunt seal. They also learn to kill the great white bear, which they sometimes meet in closer quarters than they like, as you see on next page. Bruin has evidently started out hunting himself. Perhaps he wants Eskimo meat for dinner.

The boys, too, learn to manage the curious Eskimo boat, which is so top-heavy that one needs much skill to keep right side up in it. In some places a small boat is made for a boy when he is ten years old, and he goes out with his father and takes lessons in managing it, till he becomes expert. Before he is nineteen years old, a boy is expected to kill a seal with a harpoon. You may be sure he tries his best to do it, for it is the great event of his life. A feast is made, everybody congratulates him and his parents, and the boy is now called a man.

The little girl has not been playing with dolls all this time while her brother has been getting his education. She has

TOO NEAR FOR COMFORT.

learned to sew, with a needle made from the bone of a bird's wing. She has learned to take care of the lamp, to dry the wet shoes and gloves in the net that hangs over the lamp. She has learned to cut up snow fine to made beds, to dress the skins her father and brothers bring home, and to cook the meat for dinner.

Neither of them have learned to read, nor, what is far worse, to be neat in person, for there is one dreadful thing to be said about these unfortunate little people; they never wash themselves, and never comb their hair, at least while they are young.

Captain Hall, who lived among the Eskimos, tells about trying to improve the appearance of a little Eskimo girl. After much labor, and the use of quantities of soap and water, they got at her skin, and found she was a very pretty girl, but when they took a coarse comb, and attempted to get the snarls out of her hair, they had a job! It had never been combed, and it was full of bits of moss, seal hairs, and everything else. The little thing endured very patiently, and was then dressed in a pretty red dress, in American style, and was really a beautiful child; her name was Kimnaloo.

There's some excuse you must know for their not washing; even white men, who have spent some time among them, found it almost impossible to bathe. In the first place, strange as it may seem, water is scarce. It is only procured by melting snow, and as they have no fire but an oil lamp, and have to do all their cooking and drying wet clothes over that, you can easily see it would be hard to get water for anything but food and drink.

But there's another reason, too. Any part that is wet must be dried at once, or it will be frost-bitten. At the same time a towel once used freezes like a board, and has to be dried before it can be used again. Then drying is the trouble. The lamp can't be spared from drying mittens and shoes, and if it could the towel would be smoked and covered with soot. Besides this the people have no towels, except the skins of birds, which they keep to wipe the hands on. You see it's far more trouble for the little Eskimo to keep clean than it is for you, who have only to turn a faucet to get all the water you need.

I must tell you about the house these queer little folks live in. In summer it is a tent of skins, but in winter it is a little round hut of snow. It is really a beautiful little house before it is lived in and smoked up, made of great blocks of snow, white and almost transparent. Two men can build one in an hour, with a low entrance and a long passage for a hall, so low sometimes that one has to creep in.

Inside, the women make the beds, which are also of snow, and very comfortable, it is said. To make a bed an embankment is made, and filled up with snow cut into fine pieces. On this the furs are spread, and here the family sleep, all huddled together to keep warm.

How dreadful it seems to us, that people living in that fearfully cold climate have no fire except a lamp! Yet they manage to keep warm, and even white men who live as they do have made themselves tough enough to do without fire also.

Life is not all work, even to the grown-ups. During the long winter, if they have food laid by, they have much time on their hands, and they have games and dances like other people. They play various wrestling and jumping games, and in the proper season football, with a ball of skin stuffed with sand.

One amusement is making faces, and they certainly can make themselves look most hideous. They will draw both lips into the mouth, and stick forward the chin, till they look like the "missing link," which scientists are looking for to connect the human race with the monkeys. Then they will squint frightfully, and move the head from side to side, in a way that looks as though the neck was out of joint. To make the face utterly diabolical they open and shut one eye slowly. The one who can make the worse face is the greatest fellow. This is fun worthy of savages.

Another way to pass away the tedious hours is by a sort of ventriloquism. Two men stand facing each other, and talk in this tone, at the same time staring in such a way that it seems as if their eyes would burst out of the sockets. I hope this doesn't give the little folk the nightmare, but I should think it would.

And the mothers help the little ones over the long days; they play "cat's cradle," and make ever so many more changes than we do with the string. They make deer, whale, seal, and other animals, almost without end.

Then the Eskimos of Alaska have a very curious festival, the queerest you ever heard of. To give one of these feasts, a man will save everything he can earn or make for years. He will get together great piles of valuable skins, guns, beads by the yard, suits of clothes, and everything most desirable in Eskimo life. Sometimes he will work hard for fifteen years, for this one purpose.

When ready he calls in his friends and neighbors, and spreads the feast he has prepared. As long as the food lasts they stay, perhaps for days, and then he gives them everything he has got together, *every single thing*, and leaves himself poor!

The honor of so grand an affair is all he wants to comfort the rest of his life.

I must tell you girls about an elegant "party dress" worn by an Eskimo belle to a dance. See how much it is like ours; the dress was of the intestines of seal, split and sewed together, as I shall tell you later. This makes a transparent garment, and the young girl who wore it had trimmed it most gorgeously.

It was embroidered with colored worsted, and fringed with strings of beads.

Her trowsers were white, made of Siberian reindeer skin, embroidered and decorated with strips of wolf skin. Her hair was braided on each side with strips of wolf skin and strings of beads, and over her shoulders hung necklaces and pendents of beads. On her hands were snow-white gloves of fawn skin, which fitted nicely, and were trimmed around the wrist with wolf skin.

To complete the outfit, she held in her hand, not a bouquet, nor even a sunflower, but a long eagle feather, one in each hand, with its edges decorated with swan's-down. As she danced and sang she waved the feather in the air, and no doubt she was perfectly charming. Shouldn't you like to see her?

Their dances are very funny. By way of a band a number of women will stand in a circle, with their hands hidden under the front flaps of their jackets, and sing the music. The dancer in this dance is a man, who stands in the middle of the ring, shakes his head and flings his long hair about, throws his arms and his legs, and now and then gives a yell. The women's dance is even more odd. They kneel on the ground, and then suddenly jump to their feet, then do it again, and so on, and so on, as long as they like!

Queer things these queer people eat; seal, of course, raw or half cooked, and any other meat they can get; ducks caught while moulting, and covered with down, packed in bales, skin, down and all, so that they look like small cotton bales; and for a delicacy the contents of a dead reindeer's stomach, which even Captain Hall says is delicious.

Then in summer they have blueberries, though they grow on bushes an inch or two high, on the very edge of a snow-bank, yet they *are* blueberries, and are plenty for a short time.

The drollest thing in all Eskimo land, according to a late writer, is the Eskimo dog. The gentleman who tells their funny ways has lately been to that country, and speaks of them in an article in *Scribner's Magazine*. These useful creatures, who work hard for their masters, and indeed make it possible for people to live in that terrible cold, are, to begin with, never half fed, sometimes work for eight or ten days without food, and are always hungry. They are very curious, interested in everything, and always hoping that some one will throw them a morsel to eat.

Dear me, this isn't *droll* is it? this is cruel, and makes us wish Mr. Bergh would go up there and attend to the matter.

I'll begin again, and tell you what is amusing about them. When a party of Eskimos is moving, the dogs are loaded up with the household goods, which includes tent poles, one of which is fastened on each side of each dog. Now if he would travel straight on, as a horse, or almost any animal who bears a burden will do, he would have no trouble, but that is not a dog's way.

Dogs will be dogs, even where they have to work for their living, and so these poor fellows go prowling around, as though they had no loads, smelling of every stone, and looking into every unusual object they pass. This gets the long poles terribly mixed up; sometimes half a dozen will get into a snarl, and have to be untangled, sometimes one stick will get in front and get fastened in the ground, while the other behind holds equally well. The dog is then a fixture, and can't move either way, till his yells bring some one to help.

Often they get into fights, and the loads get broken open, and if they are eatable, are quickly disposed of. There is in every pack one bully who seizes everything eatable which any other dog is lucky enough to get and of whom all the rest are afraid.

It is the great aim, says this writer, of every Eskimo dog to get into his master's house, where there is warmth, and above all food. Poor fellow! it is the only comfortable place he knows. But it is equally the one aim of the master to keep him out, and so he seldom enjoys it.

The greatest joy of a dog's life is to steal a bit of meat, but it is a fearful joy, for trouble follows instantly. No sooner does he appear with his treasure, than every other dog "goes for him." He starts on a dead run, the whole yelling pack behind him; he is headed off in one way, turns desperately to the other, and meets there another party, all bent on snatching away the delicious morsel he carries. He tries to get it down on the run; he whines and chokes and runs all together, and it would be very funny if it didn't make us pity the half-starved creatures who so patiently work for their masters.

In Eskimo land, as everywhere else, little people are fond of stories, and Dr. Rink has collected a good many for other little people to enjoy.

Should you like to know what sort of a story would please a party of Eskimo children, huddled around the lamp in a low snow cottage, while they munched away on raw meat, or blubber? Well, then, listen. This story has been told to them hundreds of times. It's as popular as Jack the Giant-killer, and Cinderella and the Glass Slipper are with you. It is the

"STORY OF KAGSAGSUK.

"Once upon a time, a miserable old woman with her adopted son lived on the bounty of some richer, but very cruel, families. They had a little shed to themselves that opened into the house-passage, but were never allowed to enter the main hut. The boy often slept among the dogs for the sake of warmth. Only the poorest scraps were thrown to this miserable pair, frozen meat being given them, with no knives to cut it, and they were told to use their teeth for knives. Now and then the wicked men pulled out a tooth belonging to the wretched boy, saying that he ate too much. Still, even in their misery, the mother loved her adopted child, and made him a pair of boots, and a small bird-spear, that he might play with the other children, and forget hunger and cold. But even here he had no peace. For his mates, instead of pitying him, tormented him; threw him down, rolled him in the snow, and the girls covered him with mud. Altogether, they treated him as did their elders, most shamefully.

"So the lad, who was dwarfed and ugly in body, gave up playing with other children, and went off daily by himself among the lonely hills. He wanted, above all things, to grow large and very strong. Now his foster-mother had told him how to do this. Therefore, one day, as he was standing between the high mountains, he cried aloud:

"'Lord of strength, come forth! Lord of strength, come to me!'

"At once a huge animal, an Amarok, appeared and stood beside him. He was greatly frightened, and started to run. The beast was very swift, and catching him, twisted its tail about him and threw him to the ground. Then he heard a rattling, as of bones. Again and again he was thrown down. Each time small seal-bones seemed to fall from him. The Amarok said:

"'These bones have stopped thy growth. If thou wishest to become strong, come here every day.'

"As the dwarf ran home, he felt lighter in body than ever before. He met his mates, and, as usual, they pelted him with mud, and he went to sleep among the dogs. He said not a word of what had happened; bore kicks and blows patiently, but each day crept away to visit the friendly monster. And each day he felt new life. He ran, and hurled the rocks right and left, and rejoiced in coming strength. Finally the beast could not overpower him, and thereupon told him he was able to conquer any man living. He was very happy, but still kept the secret safe.

"In the Autumn an enormous piece of drift-wood was towed in, and left on the beach. None could remove it. During the night the lad stole down and bore it on his shoulders to the village. In the morning all were amazed at the deed, but none could guess who did it. All this time the quiet boy endured every hardship from the people. When winter set in none could go out hunting. By and by they were in danger of starving. One day word came that three bears were in sight on an iceberg. All wished the flesh, but none dared be the first in the attack. Then the ragged Kagsagsuk put on his mother's boots, ran through the crowd, his heels almost touching his neck, and climbed the iceberg easily. The bears raised their powerful paws, but he made himself 'hard' by magic, and one by one killed them, and threw them among the astonished bystanders.

The bear-skins he gave to his mother, and ordered the flesh to be cooked.

"By this time all were extremely civil to the poor lad. The best of everything was offered him, while the men trembled before him. Each one had some present to make as a peace-offering. After supper he easily seized and crushed or tore in pieces all who had treated him badly, but saved those who had been kind to him. Afterwards he sailed far up and down the coasts, and was the greatest hunter in the tribe, and a terror to man and beast."

How do you like that? If you think little Kagsagsuk's revenge was cruel, you must remember how he was brought up, and the savage tribe he belonged to. Your stories should teach you better; do they?

CHAPTER XII.

BABIES AWAY UP IN THE CORNER; THE LITTLE TUSKI.

AWAY up in the very tip-top corner of Asia, so far east that it almost touches the western half of the world, lives a jolly little soul, which, according to the geography, we must call a Tchutski baby.

You'll be glad to hear, the first thing, that an English officer, Lieutenant Hooper, who spent nearly a year among these people, learned to talk with them, and of course knows better than the geography, says the name should be Tuski.

Tuski let it be then, and queer ways the little people of this queer name have, I can tell you. Droll-looking little round bundles of fur they are, with wide, yellowish faces, and merry black eyes.

The Tuski girl dresses exactly like her mamma in a garment which we may call a dress, a hood, or a pair of trowsers, or whichever we like, for it is all three in one. It is made of skin with the hair outside. The hood has a border of wolf or dog-skin, which is considered very elegant, and when thrown back off the head this border looks like a very odd sort of fur collar standing up around the neck.

If the girl's parents belong to the well-to-do classes, her dress is of reindeer or fawn-skin, but if they are poor, she has to content herself with seal skin, poor thing! From the neck her dress is very full, and hangs in folds, but is drawn in about the knees with what you might call trowsers, and up over the edge of these come the long fur boots, or moccasins.

She is very comfortable you see, and she is also in fashion, for she wears her hair banged!

If she goes out in the snow, that is if she is obliged to go far, she wears a cloak. This is a funny-looking thing, very thin, and almost transparent, and looks about as warm as one of gauze. It isn't for warmth, however, it is to keep the snow and the wet from reaching her furs; it is in fact a sort of waterproof, and deserves the name of "gossamer waterproof" if any such does.

It is made of the intestines of seals or some other marine animal, which looks, as perhaps you know, like the extremely thin rubber of a toy balloon, or like a bladder. When cut open, these are in long strips like narrow ribbon, and they have to be carefully sewed together to make the cloaks. Sometimes between the strips are sewed narrow fringes of fur, or bright-colored material which makes them gay.

Not only the girls wear these cloaks, but the boys, and the men and the women; and really, without them, traveling would be almost impossible. Why? well, I'm sure you'd never guess the reason, though if you had the misfortune to take a ride in that land of snow and wind, you'd soon find out. They are to keep the snow from getting into the fur of their clothes. Snow when dry and light, as it is there, gets among the hairs, clogs up, and soon loads a person down so heavily that he can hardly stand. So every one that goes out of the house wraps up in a big cloak, and keeps dry.

The Tuski boys dress differently. They wear two caps of fur, a shirt of fur with the hair inside, then a large coat, or rather a frock of deer-skin reaching to the knees. Their trowsers reach to the ankle, and are tied around the waist by a gathering-string. Ah, boys, pity them! the little Tuski can never know the delight of his first pair of suspenders.

But then we must not forget that dressing like a man has no particular charm for him, for he always dresses exactly like his father. There are no "knickerbockers" to be out-grown, no jackets or buttoned blouses to be discarded for vest and coat. He's a little man from the very first.

There is one thing he has, which his father has not, and that is a fur cushion at the back of his head, to protect him in case he falls, and as a support. But that is only while he is a baby, and cannot walk very well,

Coming up over his trowsers are his moccasins or boots, made of the skin from the leg of the reindeer, with soles of seal or walrus hide. Mittens and belt finish his dress. The most elegant garment he can hope to have is of dogskin, with long, silky, jet-black hair.

Of course he must have his hair cut off the top of his head [that's why he needs two caps I suppose]. The whole top of his head, to be in style, must be bare, but a fringe about three inches deep may be allowed to grow all around the head just where it would come out from under one of your caps.

All this is outdoors; in the house it is different, though they never have what we should call a fire. They have nothing to keep them warm or to cook with, except an oil lamp!

This sounds badly I must say, but you may save your pity. The Tuski little folk do not suffer with cold. In fact their rooms are exceedingly warm, hot you may say, since the thermometer often goes up to 100°, and that we call terrible heat in summer.

And only a lamp! (I almost hear you say.) Yes truly, only a lamp; but a very good one as you can guess, and a curious house, the oddest we've heard of yet. It is made entirely of skins. Outside and inside, floors and roof, doors and windows, walls, partitions, and beds, each and all of skins.

A tent? surely; but a strange one. It is made, outside, of walrus hide, but prepared in such a way that it is not only soft and thick, but lets a good deal of light through. "Semi-lucent" Hooper calls it, and that is so light that they need no windows, that's almost like a glass [ground glass] house, isn't it?

Let us suppose our Tuski youngster has a rich father, and a large family. His tent will be of good size, perhaps thirty or forty feet in diameter, and round in shape, so that the snow will not drift about the corners, nor the winds find any hold by which to blow it over. The wind of that country, by the way, is more terrible than you can imagine.

The walrus skin wall of the house is held up by a frame of bones! Truly, the great ribs of whales, stuck in the ground, and resting at the top on one or two props. To this frame the skin cover is fitted, and sewed nicely to shape, and a skin door makes the outside complete, except a banking up of snow to keep the air out, and help hold it against the wind.

But the inside is the oddest. In most tents, you know, the inside is all one room with the fire in the middle. In the Tuski tent, the middle is only the front hall you may say, the place where food is stored, and dog teams unharnessed, where sledges are unloaded, and heavy work is done, and property housed.

The rooms to live in are in a row around the wall, and remind one of the stalls for locomotives in a railroad "round house." Each room is in fact a sort of stall, built of skins of course, and having its own roof and walls, and its own door. It is six or eight feet deep, and, if the house belongs to a chief, it is high enough to stand up in. If it belongs to a poorer man the rooms may only be high enough to sit up in, say three feet.

You must remember that in each of these "cubby-holes" lives a mother and her children, not to count the father There all the meals are cooked and eaten, here the children play, and the mother sews, here they all sleep at night Ugh! how dreadful!

Yet it suits them. You can see now how one lamp will make a room uncomfortably warm, so that the grown-ups throw back their fur clothes, and the children throw theirs nearly all off. And you can see that chairs and tables, bedsteads and bureaus are not wanted here. The floor, neatly covered with walrus skin, is chair and bedstead and table, and certain swinging shelves overhead are bureau, trunk, and clothes-horse.

Outside in the big room, the roof of those little stalls looks like a hay mow, for hay or dried grass is piled up there to keep out cold.

The lamp which warms and lights and cooks for this house of skins, is a dish of an oval shape filled with oil, and a row of bits of moss, called "weet-o-weet," through the middle. It is a soft, beautiful light, and when well trimmed, has no smoke and no odor, but immense heat. And not a man or a boy ever is allowed to touch it, while a girl is carefully taught, for the lamp is the woman's charge.

Dinner-time comes, and what shall this queer family eat? Let me tell you what they gave to a guest, whom they wanted to be very polite to. The party sat around on the floor, and the lady of the house brought in a dish of frozen fish, to begin the meal.

The natives crunched them down as though they were nice,

but the guest, finding that the fish was not prepared according to our notions, could not eat it.

This course being finished, the wooden dish was cleaned by a scrape with the fingers of the hostess, and the next one brought on. This was even more unpleasant than the first, being the contents of the reindeer's stomach, cut in slices, and eaten with blubber. This too the Tuski family devoured with relish.

Next came boiled meat, seal and walrus, which was not bad, and after it another peculiar Tuski delicacy. It was the thick black skin of the whale, cut in small squares, and the guest found it very nice, crisp, and tasting like cocoanut. The next course was boiled reindeer flesh ; and lastly, as the greatest treat in all Tuski land, a dish of the gums of a whale, in which the ends of the whalebone could still be seen. Much to his surprise, the English gentleman found this to be really delicious, with the flavor of cream cheese.

After dinner came smoking, and then a long drink from the water-cask, when each man swallowed as much as two quarts, the traveler says.

Besides the enormous meals they eat, the people have a curious habit of munching snow or ice. They keep vessels of it in the tents, and nearly all the time are nibbling at it, between meals.

When bed-time comes for the little Tuski, the mother spreads a pile of soft skins for each one ; if she has guests she hangs curtains of skins around the bed, and everybody wraps himself up in his furs, tucks the edges of the curtains under his skin bed, and goes to sleep, if he can. Then the careful mother hangs all the wet moccasins, the soaked mittens, and everything needed to be dried, in the lattice shelves overhead, and goes to her own private pile of skins to sleep. The dogs huddle together in the outside room, the door of the tent is closed, and the Tuski house, or yarang, is ready for the long, cold night.

I'm afraid you don't see how the little people can have a very nice time, living higglety-pigglety, we may say, in little stalls around the wall. But they do. They have plays, and toys. The girls have dolls, of course, for which they make clothes like their own, that will come off. They play Tuski life with their dear pets, as you play American life with yours. They have toys carved out of ivory, and they have embroidery.

Of embroidery the little black-eyed girls are very fond. They decorate not only the cloaks I spoke of, but caps and mittens, and belts for father and brothers; even the side seams of their fur boots are aften ornamented in this way.

Their embroidery is not like yours; no silk or crewel, no gold thread or beads go to this fancy work, away up in the corner of Asia. Reindeer hair dyed in bright colors, and bits of leather and fur (also sometimes dyed) cut into fancy shapes and sewed on, or put together like a sort of patchwork; these are the materials of which the Tuski girl makes her pretty things. Then she has the dance, which Hooper tells about.

The dances of these queer little bundles of fur are extremely funny. In one dance a long row of girls took hold of hands, and moved to the sound of a sort of two stringed fiddle which they have. They began with mincing steps, and droll twists of the arms and head. First the middle of the line danced backwards, while the ends kept in place, till the line was the shape of a semi-circle. Then the middle came back to place, and the two ends danced backwards till the semi-circle turned the other way.

Then the line came up straight again, and all together moved forward a few steps, and then all back a few steps. After doing this several times they separated, and quietly formed again behind the player, as if to surprise him. This they did two or three times, and the dance was done.

But the most amusing dance was performed by three little girls, and is a very common play among the children. They stood up in a row, with toes turned in, and hands hidden in the opposite sleeves, and played a lively sort of pantomime. The middle one turned first to one and then to the other, and seemed to now coax them on, and now drive them away, while the two outside ones gave little sidewise jumps, at one moment turning the face towards the middle one, and the next moment turning away.

All the time they were slowly chanting a song, and suddenly, at the end of the verse, all three jumped entirely around, saying:

"Um! um! um!" in a satisfied tone, and then threw their bodies into three extraordinary contortions, which the gentleman who describes the play cannot describe, yet were the funniest he ever saw, and always made him shout with laughter. The chant was about the rabbit and the ermine, and he thinks the dance in some way told the story of the chase and catching of poor bunny. The "um!" was probably the grunt of pleasure of the naughty ermine, and the queer movement after it may be in imitation of the rabbit's wriggling to get away.

The boys also have their toys and plays. They have little sledges, and all sorts of animals cut from ivory. Then they have wrestling and running games. They sit on the floor two of them, feet against feet, and try to pull each other over; or they squat opposite each other and try the same thing. Funniest of all, they put one band around their two necks, and try to pull each other over by leaning back. Big boys and even men try these games.

They have many gymnastic feats, jumping distances, and also jumping into the air and kicking a bar off, and other ways of amusing themselves.

Then the grown-ups have a sort of theatrical entertainment, which the little people also enjoy, for there's no such thing in Tuski land as shutting up the youngsters in the nursery while father and mother go out; where the big folks go, there also go the little ones.

The thing they are most fond of in their performances is an imitation of the manners and customs of their neighbors the Eskimos. Though the latter belong to America, and the Tuski to Asia, they are separated only by a narrow strait, as you'll see if you look on your map of Asia.

No doubt Eskimo ways seem to them very droll, and the man who can imitate them is sure of an audience and plenty of fun. He dresses like them, even to wearing only one mitten, which is a custom among Eskimos, and he mimics their voice and their tone.

Then, while the musicians are making as much noise as they can, with fiddles and drums, he goes through the whole round of Eskimo life, paddling in a canoe, hunting for an enemy, eating and drinking and fighting. Even his hunts are imitated—catching a whale in which part of the time the actor is the Eskimo, and part of the time he's the whale.

All through the play, which of course is meant to make fun of their neighbors, the Tuskies applaud, crying :

"Kah! Kah! Kah!"

And from beginning to end is a low sort of gurgle of satisfaction, and a constant talk, not so very different from our entertainments after all, you see.

Besides this there are dancing, or rather posturing to music, where the feet are not moved, and of course story-telling. It would be hard to find a spot in Asia where story-telling was not one of the best-loved entertainments.

When the little Tuski goes out to ride it is on a sledge drawn by reindeer, with lines from the horns, or by six or eight dogs running side by side. If there are sharp particles of ice on the crust of snow, as is often the case, the dogs must have on their overshoes, little funny leather ones, tied on with shoestrings. These poor creatures—the dogs—have a hard life, and are often treated cruelly. They are fed very little, and often go three or four days without a morsel to eat. When traveling, and the traveler is buried in his furs to sleep, the wretched dogs have to burrow into the snow to keep from freezing.

When the traveler reaches a tent, he is instantly made welcome, even if he doesn't bring letters of introduction with him. A dish of frozen fish is set before him, and, as soon as it can be made ready, a warm meal.

When a party of Tuski visited the ship of the English party of whose doings Lieutenant Hooper writes, they were somewhat embarrassed to entertain them. For the ordinary English dishes—preserved meats and such things—the Tuski had a great contempt, but a tallow candle was a sweet morsel, to be eaten like a banana, and off the blubber the ship kept for the dogs, they made a good meal.

There was one treat the English could give them, however,

and that was a lump of sugar. But they had the funniest way of eating it that you ever heard of. They would roll the lump in a piece of tobacco leaf, put it carefully in their cheek, and hold it there till it dissolved! This sweet morsel they call *laloop*, and it was the choicest they ever knew.

The magnet was a great mystery to them, and they thought the owner of one was a wizard. A man who could make a bit of iron lift up other iron things, and above all could make needles dance about it, could do any uncanny thing he wanted to, they were perfectly sure.

Perhaps nothing the English had so much delighted them (at any rate the woman who had the lamps to light) as matches. The poor Tuski woman, to light her lamp, works eight or ten minutes very hard, twirling a stick in a hole in a piece of wood, before she gets a spark, and the instant light of the match was a miracle to her. The gift of half a dozen matches was to her a royal present, and called forth blessings on the head of the giver.

CHAPTER XIII.

THE LITTLE OLD MAN BABY; THE CHINESE.

THE little old man baby lives in the queerest country in the world, where the bald-headed baby looks like his grandfather, and the grown-up ladies can't walk (to speak of).

Everything in that strange land is the wrong way, to us, and it is enough to drive one crazy to be suddenly set down in one of their queer cities. Their wheelbarrows have sails, and their pigs ride to market in a basket; their books begin where ours end, read backward, have the title on the front edge, and foot-notes at the top of the page; their carpenters sit down and work towards themselves, instead of from themselves, as ours; and so far from drawing near to the stove to get warm, each one carries his own stove about in his hands or in his sleeve; they have no Sunday, and they dun a man by carrying off his front door, to keep till he pays up. Their signs stand on end, and they keep on their caps to be polite.

This land of queer things is China, and it is full of wonders for us. Here is a picture of the wheelbarrow with a sail. It shows a family on a journey, and though it has a sail, you see it is so loaded that it takes a donkey to pull, and papa himself to push, to get it along. Mamma and the baby, and the little daughter, ride with the baggage, the son rides the donkey, and only the father and the dog walk.

If you should see the droll little yellow-skinned baby, with his eyes set in bias, strapped tight to the back of an older brother or sister, and jouncing around the street as its careless nurse plays, or runs, or jumps about, you would think, wouldn't you, that babies weren't much prized in China?

WHEELBARROW WITH A SAIL.

But you would be greatly mistaken, for nowhere on this round globe of ours is there so much rigmarole, and so many ceremonies over a youngster as in China, unless, indeed, a family has more of them than it wants. In that case they simply drown the new-comer, as we drown a superfluous kitten.

The first thing done is a ceremony to keep baby from being frightened by anything; and when you come to see the frightful things the Chinese delight in, you'll think this a very necessary performance with the little Chinese.

It is a solemn affair. On a piece of red paper are written two words, and in the paper are folded several articles: two of the fruits used for soap, to ensure that baby shall be a neat and tidy person; some pith of a rush used in writing, to make him fortunate in life; one or two onions, to make him intelligent; two pieces of charcoal, that he may be strong; a lock of hair from a cat, and another from a dog, to prevent him from being frightened by the noises of these animals.

This collection of articles is wrapped in the red paper, tied with a red string, and hung outside the nursery door as a charm.

Even then, however, the little yellow baby isn't safe; precautions must be taken inside. A pair of papa's pantaloons must be hung on the bedstead, with the waist part lowest (upside down). Upon these is put a paper in which is written the request that all bad influences will kindly go into the garment, instead of troubling baby.

They can't be so bad as people pretend, I'm sure, if they'll heed this request.

But there's a worse evil than being frightened that threatens the China baby (not to speak of other youngsters), and that is the danger that he may be a thief, or a meddler, or, worst of all, disobedient!

You may think this is hard to prevent in so young a person, but nothing is easier to a Chinese. A bit of red cord, and perhaps a few cash (or small pieces of money) are all that is necessary. The cord, with the cash strung on it, is tied around his wrists, either connecting the two, or each one separate. Quite simple, you see!

These serious matters all carefully attended to, the Chinese baby may be considered safe for a week or two, and then the charms are taken away.

At one month old, the little fellow makes the acquaintance of a person whom he can never do without as long as he lives, that is, if he happens to be a boy. This is the barber, who shaves the poor little head of both girl and boy, though the girl dispenses with his services after a while.

This first shave is a great occasion; friends are invited, and a feast given, and the youngster gets a name. It is not for life, as yours is, it is only to last till he goes to school, and it is called his "milk name." The name may be Rose, or Jasmine, or Patience, or Number One, or Number Two, or any other fanciful name.

After this shaving there is allowed to grow on boys a little fringe on the back of the head to begin the cue, which as soon as possible is gummed up, and tied with red silk into a baby pigtail an inch long, and sticks straight out from the head in a very droll way, as you see in this picture of three children at play. The boy in the middle shows the little cue. This funny picture was made by a Chinese artist. Jolly babies, aren't they?

Now the little Chinese, being well protected by charms to keep off evil, is allowed to live in peace till he gets to be four months old, when there comes another feast, and another great ceremony. The child is taught to sit in a chair!

For this important occasion his grandmother provides a curious-looking chair, painted red, and a quantity of sticky candy. It must be *very* sticky, for it is put in the chair and baby seated upon it, and it serves to keep him from slipping out, and get him used to sitting up straight! Queer ways among these "Celestial" neighbors of ours.

HAVING A GOOD TIME.

This first baby-chair is sometimes gilded, playthings are hung up to amuse the solemn-faced little old man, and he is now expected to content himself with seeing life from his own chair.

The next great day in his life comes when he is a year old, and, unconscious baby as he is, he decides the occupation of his whole life. A feast is made, and friends are invited to see him make his choice, which he does in a genuine Chinese way, of course.

It is a sort of object-lesson. A large bamboo sieve is brought in, in which are several things—a set of money-scales, a pair of shears, a foot measure, a brass mirror, a pencil, ink, paper, a book or two, the Abacus (or counting machine, of balls strung on wires in a frame), some silver or gold ornaments, fruits, and other things. Why so many? Because when one has to choose for life he needs a variety.

The sieve, with its curious contents, is placed on the table, and the black-eyed baby, in span-new garments, is seated in the sieve, with all these treasures before him.

Now is the fateful moment; his friends hang breathless on his decision. All these objects are within reach of his hand, and the one he takes up decides his fate, because they think it shows his natural tastes.

If he takes up a book, or pen, he is destined to be a scholar, and will be educated for it; if the money-scales attract his baby eyes, or the silver or gold, his fate is to make money; if the fruit is the object of his choice, alas, he will be greedy; and if the mirror, vain! History does not say what is done with the unfortunate baby who shows a dreadful tendency to greediness by selecting fruit, or to vanity by the attraction of a bright mirror, but I suppose the parents are mortified and grieved, and no doubt they have some powerful charm which will correct the evil in their beloved baby.

While very young the little Chinese is taught "manners," how to come into a room, to bow very low to parents or those older than himself, even till his head nearly touches the floor, and to "chin-chin." This is their polite greeting, taking the place of our hand-shaking. It looks funny enough, for it is a sort of shaking hands with one's self. The hands are doubled up like fists, put together and shaken at the person to be greeted.

The child also learns great deference for his parents, and calls his father "Family's Majesty" or "Venerable Father" instead of simply "Papa," like you ignorant western barbarians.

The dress of the boy about this time, and forever after, is like his grandfather's, and he looks like the venerable old gentleman seen through the wrong end of a spy-glass. If he belongs to a rich family, the dress is of rich material and gay colors, and if to a poor one, it is the same shape but of coarse stuff. Around his neck he wears charms to keep him from danger and evil.

The China girl wears also jacket and trowsers of gay colors, with bangles and chains and many ornaments. She wears her hair down her back in one or two braids, and over her forehead she has—bangs! For full dress she may have her hair gilded. That is horrid, you think, but wait till I tell you how the mammas arrange their hair!

But the youngsters grow, school days come. Now the boy takes his books—no! excuse me—he takes no books, he is fitted out with a curious set of school things. Two small candles! a few sticks of incense!! and a little paper mock-money!!!

Books are respected in his school, but more important is "deportment." He must learn how to behave to parents, to strangers, on all occasions. He must learn to walk through the streets, and a thousand other things. Above all he must burn incense and mock-money before the figure of Confucius, whom the Chinese honor as their greatest wise man.

Ah, the poor little Chinese! School is a hard place for him.

He goes as early in the morning as he can see to read; at breakfast-time, if he knows his lesson, he goes home and eats that meal and returns to the school-room till night, or it is too dark to see.

Now he has a new name, his school name, and a queer one too; it may be "Ink-grinder" or "Promising study" or "Entering virtue," or some other equally appropriate.

After six months of training in behavior, he begins books; not A-B-C books, like yours. No indeed! the unfortunate little Chinese plunges at once into the biggest and wisest book, that takes the wisdom of men to understand. He begins on Confucius. Each Chinese character is a word, and before he can read tolerably he must be familiar with three thousand of them.

See him as he goes to school with books enough for a bigger boy. Now you can see his cue is a good deal longer. And here, too, is the Chinese girl with her bangs, and her funny cap. (See title page.)

In school, each scholar studies at the top of his voice, swaying back and forth undisturbed by the babel around him, and he recites standing with his back to the teacher. After he has gone through Confucius, and another work of the same sort, which takes three or four years, he can go to college if he likes, and if he was so unfortunate as to take up a book when he sat in his bamboo sieve, I suppose he will have to do it.

If the teacher wishes to give the pupils a treat, he invites them, not to a picnic or an excursion, but to a feast in honor of Confucius. He gives each boy a white paper fan, on which is written a quotation from the Chinese wise books, and perhaps also to each one a toy.

When you see the sort of teacher the little Chinese has, you will not be surprised at any queer thing he may do. Here he is.

SCHOOLMASTER

How different the school days of the little China boy from yours! You pity him, and think he has a hard time; let me tell you about the girls.

The child-life of a Chinese girl of the higher classes is a long, long agony of pain so great that many prefer to die. All for the purpose of having what we consider a deformity, little feet; so small that their owners cannot walk, except in a tottering manner, holding on to something.

While still very young the poor girl's feet are bandaged with long narrow strips of muslin, which draw the toes down under the sole, and make, after years of suffering, a foot of three or four inches long, with a sort of club foot above it.

From earliest infancy, a twelve-year-old bride told Mrs. Feudge her sufferings had been unspeakable. She often became frantic and tore off the bandages, and when they were put on again she would become delirious. After five or six years the pain gradually grew less, and at that age she did not think much about it except when the bandages were taken off, when the torture was worse than she could say.

Yet, how dreadful the power of custom! without this deformity no Chinese lady could enter society, and no Chinese gentleman would take her for a wife. She goes tottering through life carried about in a chair, or on the back of her maid, who holds her hands behind her, to receive her mistress's knees; and so she is very aristocratic and elegant, and helpless, and her friends are proud of her. The Chinese girl has no "young lady" life. How could she? She is married at twelve years, and jumps from her dolls to wifehood. The marriage is, as with all the army of Asiatic girls, arranged by her parents.

When the matter is announced to the child, her bangs are brushed back, and her hair is "done up."

Now this is a curious affair, and I want to tell you about it. It is drawn back from the forehead, made stiff with gum, and then piled up in a wonderful mass of bows, and loops, and wings, and rolls, all so firm with the gum that they stay where put, and need no hairpins. The whole outside is in perfect order; such a thing as mussy hair is unknown.

This structure lasts a week! and is adorned with flowers or jewels, for dress occasions, and the miserable owner sleeps with a leather pillow under her neck, or packs her whole head safely away in a box. I should think she'd want to take it off, as well as her feet.

From the time our little girl is engaged, even if it were when she was a baby, as is sometimes done, she has to "turn over a new leaf," you may say, in her manners. She must see no company at home, and if she goes out she goes in a close sedan chair. She must even be very reserved with her own brothers.

Then, before the wedding day, the bridegroom receives another new name, with a feast and ceremonies, of course.

The things that have to be done, the charms to keep away evil, the ceremonies, the processions, and the thousand other performances that have to be gone through to marry our China boy and girl, are something appalling. And they're not sure till the very last minute that they will really be married, for if they happen to do anything unlucky, as break a dish, or lose something, the whole thing comes to an end.

If everything goes off right, the girl goes at last in a red sedan chair to her husband's house, to the home of his father and mother, where she becomes their slave and drudge for the rest of her life. They may punish her by whipping, even publicly, and they may put her in a cage in the street for everybody to see, with a sign to hold her up to utmost contempt of everybody. "Unfilial." If still she is not obedient, they may whip her to death, and nobody interferes.

The wedding calls are as different from ours, as everything else they do. First the gentlemen come in, and the young husband praises his wife, mentions her little feet, and her delicate hands, and so on, and then he invites them into another room for refreshments. The ladies then come in, and they set themselves to making remarks, criticising the bride, and saying unpleasant things. The object is to try her temper. If she keeps good-natured, her reputation is made for life; but if she gets angry, she is always considered bad-tempered.

No wonder girl babies are often drowned or given away. The cost of marrying one is so enormous that only the rich can do it properly. The parents have the care and expense of bringing her up, and then she is married, and lost to them.

This picture shows a young China girl, with her newly married husband. She does not belong to the upper class, because, you see, she has full-sized feet. But see her curious dress, and her head decoration.

Oh dear! let's go back to the little people. The last ceremony of childhood is "going through the door" to man and womanhood. It is a very imposing affair.

The door is a tall frame of bamboo, like door-posts, and it is set in the middle of the floor. There are priests and musicians; there is a procession led by a priest with a horn, and through the door goes solemnly the youth or maiden after him.

The door is placed in each corner of the room, one after another, and the procession winds around and goes through it again and again. Now the child is of age, but don't fancy that he, or she, can do as he likes. Never, so long as his father or

JUST MARRIED.

mother lives can a Chinaman do as he likes. He must do as they say in everything, or be punished. Unfilial conduct is one of the worst of crimes in China. His wages go to them, his business is managed by them, however old, and however unreasonable they may be.

But although the little Chinese is taught not to romp and play undignified games, though his school life is hard, and he can never do as he likes, still he has lots of fun.

In the first place he has many sorts of street shows, marionettes, or dancing dolls, which spin around, flourish their arms, and in various ways amuse the youngsters who crowd around to see; peep-shows, where he can look into a hole in a box and see wonderful things; and shadow puppets, who swallow knives, turn somersets, and do other strange things.

Here you see one of these puppet-shows. The feet on the bench show that a man is behind the curtains, and working the shadows. How interested the people look! not only the little folk, but big ones as well; even a woman with her fine fan has stopped to see the wonder.

Then there are street processions on the birthdays of popular Chinese gods. One is a stilt performance, where men dress in fantastic dress, and walk through the streets singing and chanting, sometimes thrusting out one stilt into the air, and again whirling around, or otherwise showing off what they can do.

There is also the game of dragon. The dragon is an immense creature made of bamboo hoops, covered with cloth, and painted to look as a dragon is supposed to look. This object can be lighted up by lanterns inside, and it is held up on poles by boys or men, and carried around the streets. It is many feet long, and can be turned and twisted about, which makes it look very much alive.

The boys, too, play shuttlecock, with the soles of their feet. In fact, this game is more like football, as you see in this picture, which was taken from an old Chinese painting. The dress

THE SHADOW MAN.

WITH THEIR FEET.

of the boys is different from the common boys' dress nowadays, you will notice.

Another game is a lion chasing a ball. Perhaps a Chinese lion would like a ball, and, anyway, they fancy he would like to play with it as puss plays with one.

The lion is of course an immense creature, made of bamboo and cloth, and it is carried by two boys, who put their heads and shoulders inside his body, something as you American boys make an elephant with a gray blanket or shawl. Sometimes the boys' legs are painted to represent the legs of the lion. The animal has his mouth open (for the convenience of the boy inside, who must see out), and he runs after a third boy, who carries a big ball. They dodge about the streets, and make a great deal of fun.

But, above and before all, the little Chinaman has the kite. China is the headquarters of this toy, and not only boys but grown-up men spend hours flying them. They are of all sizes and shapes; men and women, dragons, bats, and butterflies, spectacles, and ships, bouquets of flowers, and pagodas, or great buildings, lighted up inside.

There are snakes that wriggle and twist, flocks of birds that fly from a hawk, trees whose fruits explode in fireworks, and kites that give out music as they fly. In fact, there's hardly an object you can think of that is not made into a kite, and put up in the air of China, and some are so large it takes three or four men to hold them.

There is a special day, the ninth day of the ninth month, specially devoted to kites, and every China boy or man in the kingdom tries to put up one of the delightful things. Sometimes as many as forty thousand people will be out on this business, or pleasure, and a hill or plain near a Chinese city must be a curious sight indeed on kite day.

There's another thing that one thinks of always as a part of a Chinaman, and that is a lantern. It is hard to tell whether more ado is made over the kite than the lantern.

TIGER OF WAR AND A BRAVE.

In the first place, every person is obliged by law to carry one at night, and the streets are filled with thousands of them, even the soldier in the ranks carries his lantern, and a Chinese soldier is a curious object even without a lantern, as you see in this picture of "a Tiger of war and a Brave."

A lantern-shop is an interesting place to go to, and people are there in crowds, especially at the time of the Feast of Lanterns. When one has made a purchase in this crowded shop, and wants to get out without smashing his fragile lantern, he hoists it on a pole, and squeezes out through the mass.

They have lanterns of all shapes and sorts, in greater variety even than the kites. They have them in the shape of animals, and men; some roll on the ground and keep lighted; some gallop like a horse, and others whirl like a top. There are ships that sail, and soldiers that march.

In all these performances the hot air, heated by the candle inside, is the power that makes them go.

Some lanterns are made of red paper with patterns in holes; others are elegantly painted; some are carried in the hand, others hung on the wall. The most costly are covered with silk gauze, and beautifully painted.

The Feast of Lanterns comes on the first full moon of the year, and is a great occasion, when everybody hangs lanterns of various kinds before his door, and all the house is lighted up. There are processions, music, and fireworks, of course, for these three things are a part of almost every Chinese merrymaking.

Another amusement, though perhaps it is more for the grown-ups, is the theater, and it is so odd that I must tell you about it. If there is no regular building for it, temporary sheds or light buildings are put up for the purpose; a great crowd collects, and the play begins. The stage is a simple affair, and the acting is more like child's play than like an entertainment for grown-up people.

For instance, if a man is sent off on horseback to deliver a message, he will take a whip, pretend to mount a horse, and gallop across the stage. When he reaches the other side he stops, and cries out that he has got there, and delivers his message. Ghosts or other supernatural creatures come up through a big trap-door, and if they feel like it, call for help to get up. There's not even an attempt to delude anybody, which we in our theaters take such pains to do.

But the funniest is yet to be told; the play lasts three days and nights! They do not sit there every moment; the audience has now and then a recess for eating or sleeping. We should think they would be tired out, but on the contrary they are so interested that they stay away as short a time as possible.

They are fond of bringing in characters we never meddle with, as the sun and moon. The persons who take these characters represent it by some sign, as a moon on a pole, or a figure to represent the sun. The female parts are played by boys, and the dress of the actors is like nothing you ever saw, as you see in this picture.

New Year's Day is another great time, when everybody calls on his friends, or sends his cards; when everybody pays his debts, if he can, and three days are given up to having a good time.

The Chinese baby's name, as I have told you, is not for life, as yours is. He has a new one on every important occasion; besides these you have heard of he has still another if he gets into public office, which is called his official name. There's another thing about his name; he writes it backward, as we should say. As if your friend John Smith should write his name Smith John.

The Chinese girl has still another trouble about her name; when she is married she drops, not her family name as we do,

PERFORMERS.

but her own name. Suppose Mary Jones married John Smith, or, to speak Chinese fashion, Jones Mary married Smith John. Her married name would be Smith Jones Mrs., not Mrs. Mary Smith, as with us. Isn't that funny to our notions?

Now, how does the Chinese youngster eat? We've been hearing about some very queer modes of eating since we began to hunt out the ways of little people.

RATS FOR SALE.

Well, he doesn't eat on the floor like other little Asiatics, though he does eat strange things. Neither does he eat with his fingers, but with a pair of "nimble lads," which we call chopsticks. These are simply two small sticks, which may be of bamboo, ivory, or gold, as he can afford. Each person has his own, and may carry them in an elegant case hung to his waist.

Though they eat at a table, it is not like our dinner. The dishes are placed in a sort of pyramid, and everything is cut to small bits. That is necessary, indeed, when there are no knives or forks. Our way of eating meat at the table they regard as barbarous, as in fact they do most of our ways.

They eat meat and vegetables, especially rice; almost everything that we do, and some that we do not, as puppies, kittens, and rats. Here is a Chinese picture showing the peddler of rats. But their great delight, their tip-top luxury, is watermelon seeds. These are sold everywhere; in the villages, on the streets, and everywhere; junks on the rivers will be loaded with these seeds alone. People always have them, and they munch them during business, before dinner, traveling, and everywhere they go.

In some places melons are grown almost entirely for the seeds, and in these places ripe melons will be placed on the road for every passer-by to eat, with the sole request that the seeds are left for the owner. The long nails which many wear are very handy to strip off the shell of the precious seeds, and it looks very funny to see grave Chinamen at the business.

On page 331 is a girl with fresh vegetables for sale. Her two pretty baskets, hung from a bamboo pole, don't look much like our vegetable peddlers with carts or great ugly baskets on their arms or heads (if they happen to be German). See what a fine shade hat she has, like a parasol with a hook on top.

The place in which the little "celestial" lives is as interesting as anything about him. No broad streets with name on every corner, no high blocks of buildings, no long row of residences, no horses and carriages, no street cars.

Let me tell you: in the biggest cities the most important

streets are not over ten feet wide, and many are much narrower. Then every little way the street is cut off by a gate across it, and on the gate is put the name, such as the "street of a hun-

PEDDLER OF SWEETS.

dred grandsons." Queer shapes their gates have, too; see this round one from Pekin, on page 333.

Farther on is a street in Canton, with its tall signs on both

GIRL PEDDLER.

sides. In the country the roads are often mere narrow paths, hardly wide enough for two men to pass.

The shops are all open to the street, and some of them in

TOYS FOR SALE.

Pekin are so beautiful with carving, gilding, and painting, that they look as if they ought to be kept under glass. Besides shops for everything that we have, there are lantern-shops, and others

GATE IN PEKIN.

which furnish everything for processions, of which the people are so fond—bridal or funeral processions, with the men and boys to carry things, as the bride's wardrobe, which goes in state through the streets.

The signboards stand on end in their streets, and queer ones are seen by the stranger who understands the language, such as "Black cat served hot at all hours." Why poor puss must be black is only one more Chinese mystery.

An interesting thing to watch in a Chinese city is the long string of peddlers, for almost anything can be bought of them. There is the seller of sweets, as nice to the little Chinese as your finest candies to you, on page 330; he has a box on one end of the bamboo pole which he carries across his shoulders, and a mysterious covered can on the other end, and he calls attention by beating on a gong.

There's another gong-beater. He sells toys. Look at the wonders he has in his queer-shaped basket; dolls, and carts, and balls, and tops, and flags, and dishes, and dozens of other things.

Then there is the peddler of bread, in odd little loaves like rolls or biscuit, who look droll enough sitting on the ground by their trays, as you see on page 336.

One of the strangest things to see in the streets is a a temple, or what we should call a church. See the curious decorations, the dragons on the roof, and the many signs standing each side of the door. (Page 337.)

I have shown you some other people at their prayers. Look at a Chinaman (page 338). The wheel he stands by is a Prayer Mill. Each bit of paper on the end of a spoke is a written prayer, and all he has to do is to turn the wheel around. As

STREET IN CANTON.

many times as it whirls through the air, so many times has he uttered all the prayers written on the papers. So he thinks, and you see how earnestly he does his work.

The little Chinese whose father is poor, lives in a low, one-story house, without windows, or with one opening closed by board shutters. He has no chimney, fire-place, or stove, no rugs, or mats, or carpets.

BREAD-SELLERS.

His stove to keep warm is a tiny affair, a sort of lamp which burns oil, and which he carries about in his hands or his sleeve, and the cooking range is simply a portable affair, a sort of fire-box, that can be carried into any room when it is wanted.

He needs no carpets or rugs, for he carries his own in the thick, soft soles of his shoes. You see, the idea in China is not

TEMPLE.

to be sociably comfortable, but each one for himself. So as they do everything the other way from our way, of course they keep fuel, that we store in the cellar, on the roof, and in Canton,

PRAYER MILL.

where ground-room is very scarce, they even do much housework in the same place, as well as lounge and sleep there.

But the rich little Chinese fares better. His home is very grand indeed, of marble, carved so finely that it might be jewelers' work, chairs and tables and floors of marble, and ebony, and porcelain. Fine gardens, as you see here, with artificial lakes,

IN THE GARDEN.

flowers and trees. There will be no windows to be seen, only shutters which open half the house to the air, and doors of all sorts of queer shapes, round, or leaf-shaped, or semi-circular.

Even this fine house will be of one story generally, probably because it is impossible for little feet to go up and down stairs, though here is the house of a rich man which is two stories high.

The strangest piece of furniture to be seen in the houses is, an elegant coffin, which is considered a very choice present for a child to give to his father, and is kept in a conspicuous place, where everybody can see how very filial is the giver. If the daughter of the house wishes to give an elegant present to a parent, she will embroider a beautiful white silk winding-sheet to go with it.

To take the place of door-plates, the Chinese gentleman hangs before the door a lantern with his name and title on it. The father in this elegant house will probably wear immense nails on his fingers. He will carefully tend and cultivate them, till they are several inches long, often as long as his hand, and then he may have them stained and polished to look like tortoise-shell. If he is a merchant he will look like that on page 343.

Naturally things so delicate as finger nails would easily break, so this fine gentleman protects them by long cases fitted over them, and made of silver or gold, or even of bamboo. This is the height of refinement in Chinese eyes, probably because it shows plainly that he never descends to work.

The mother indicates her elegance by her useless little feet, which they call "golden lilies," and she may spend her time in playing games of cards, being amused by various people hired for the purpose, and above all by dressing, or rather being dressed.

The house that most concerns travelers in China is the hotel, and that's the oddest yet. See one over the leaf. See the

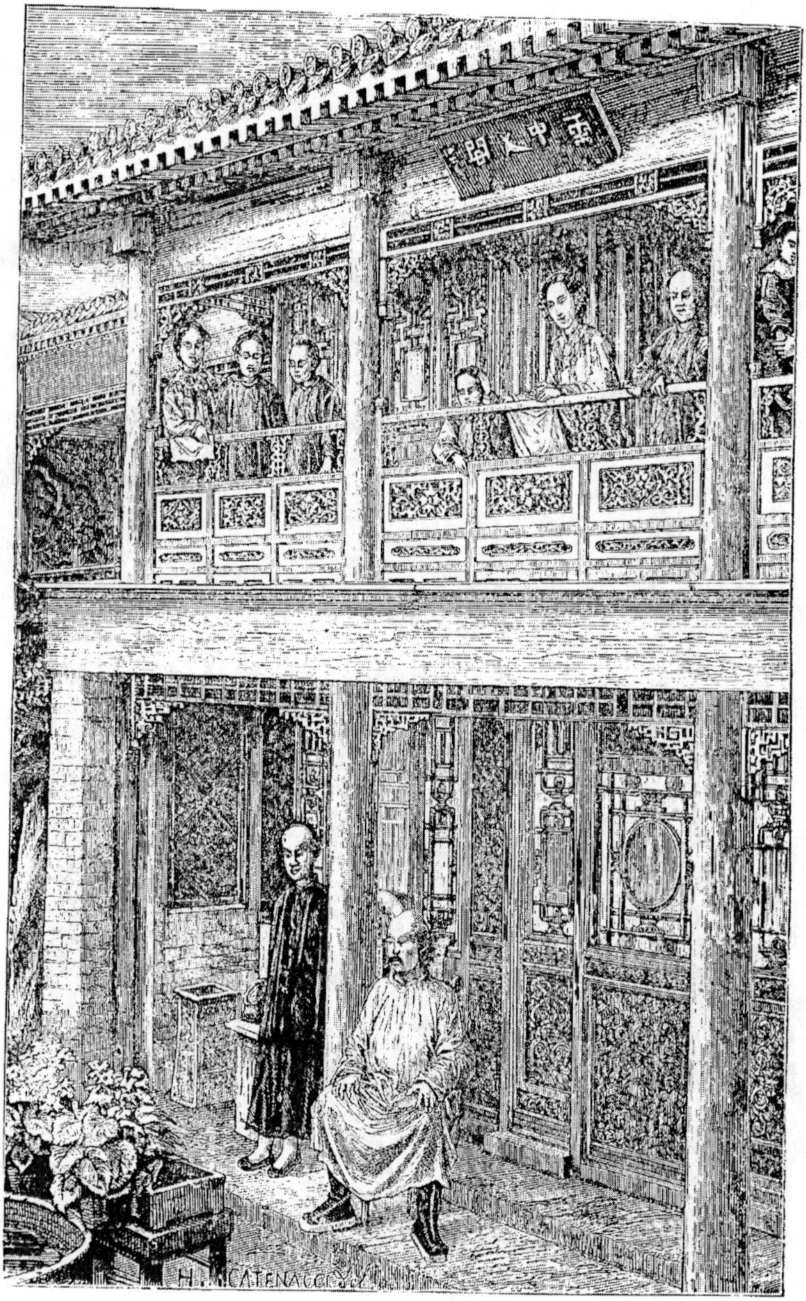

HOME OF THE LITTLE CHINESE.

curious windows, and the lantern hung up to light it. But the strangest thing about it is the brick sort of platform, which goes across the back and part way on the sides.

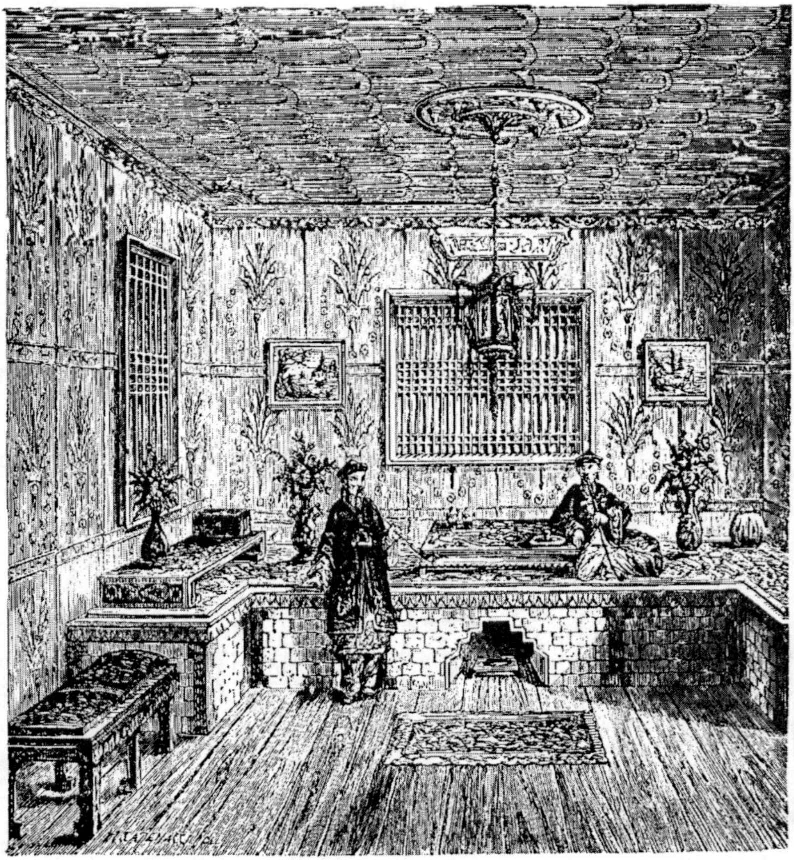

IN A HOTEL.

You may not think it, but that is the hotel bed! And worse still, the only one in the house.

At present a person, the landlord perhaps, or maybe a guest,

CHINA BOY'S PAPA.

sits there smoking; but when night comes, a great fire will be built under it to warm it up, and every traveler who comes will roll himself in his own blankets and lie down, his head to the wall, and his feet at the outside edge.

Each new-comer will join the row of human bundles, till before morning the whole bed, or kang, may be full. In the morning all will get up, some will start off on foot, and others perhaps in such a traveling carriage as this on page 346, with a driver to each horse.

But there are thousands of little people in this strange land who never live in a house at all; they live in boats. In Canton there are miles and miles of boats, making streets by themselves, and all anchored in the river. Here the babies sleep in a hole in the bottom, packed like herrings, while father, and mother, and other grown-ups occupy the seats, or shelves, that pull out of the side. Here is a boat baby in his home.

When little, these boat babies are tied by a cord to the mast, so they will not fall overboard, or sometimes wear around their necks a gourd or two, to keep their heads above water.

Others, that live by fishing, have a different kind of boat, (Page 347). What sort of fishing is this? Wouldn't it be fun, boys, to fish by simply running up and down a plank, like the China boy in the picture. When the plank goes up the net goes down, and when the boy turns and goes down, the net comes up, full of fish, sometimes.

There are other queer little folk in China; there's a girl who works for her bread, with a handkerchief tied over her head, and her big shade hat in her hand; and next is a country girl, with a queerer head-covering yet. She belongs to the Chinese island of Formosa, and is called a Pepohoan.

HOME OF THE BOAT BABIES.

The people called by this name, though really Chinese, are said to be much more sincere and simple-minded than their race in China proper, and altogether pleasanter people to live with.

TRAVELING.

On page 351 is a mother and baby. This sober little fellow, you see, rides in a sling.

There is one thing in which the little people of China (and the big ones too) beat the world, and that is in superstition. At

FISHING.

YOUNG GIRL.

least, it is to be hoped that no other people believe in such terrible things as they do. It is their settled opinion that the air is full of evil influences, whose constant endeavor is to harm them, and their whole life is full of attempts to keep them away.

CHINESE GIRL.

This is a dreadful belief. The China boy begins his baby life by wearing charms; he makes offerings to the evil spirits, he consults omens, he guides his conduct by lucky and unlucky days. He never sets his house square with his neighbor's; a pointed roof must not turn toward his house, bad influence must be kept off his roof by a porcelain cat sitting down, and looking away. Opposite an alley a post must be placed, to break the force of evil; and out of a window he hangs a basket to catch the spirit; everywhere he pastes printed prayers, in the house, on farming tools, all over the boat-houses.

Fire-crackers are a great charm to frighten off evil, and are used on every occasion. The Chinese classics are a charm when placed under the pillow, and a mirror hung on the house outside will reflect back the evil. Under the door-sill are placed coins, and on the junks are painted eyes, to scare the monsters of the deep.

One hardly knows whether to laugh at the childishness of these notions, or to pity a nation which believes them.

If a child is delicate, they try to cheat the evil spirit, which they think is tormenting him, in several equally curious ways. They wish to make the spirit think that he is not very important, and it is not worth his while to bother about that child. So they sometimes make him wear a hideous mask, and sometimes pretend to give him away, that they care so little for him, that he now belongs to some one else; and really and truly, children, some friends will take the boy home, as though he belonged to them.

If that does not cure him, they try the Hundred Families' Lock. This is done by the father, who collects from a hundred families a few cash each. With this money he buys a silver lock, which is hung by a chain around the child's neck. Thus each of the hundred families has a hold on him to "lock him to life."

IN A SLING.

When the China boy's father and mother are dead, you may think he is relieved from the duties to them that are so important during their life. Little do you know of their ingenuity; they still keep them supplied with clothes and furniture, servants, and everything they think they can need in that unseen world to which they have gone.

But how do they send them? That would be a poser to us, ignorant barbarians that we are! But it has no difficulties to a Chinese mind. The friends are invisible, of course the gifts must be invisible, and no way so quickly makes them so as burning; so the gifts are burnt. But being burnt, paper is as good as cloth, so reason these filial children. So they buy the garments, etc., made of paper, pack them in a big trunk, or a wardrobe made of bamboo and paper, touch a light to it, and think they have made a valuable present to their dead parents or friends. Millions of dollars' worth are burnt up in this way every year, it is said.

The geography that the little people of China learn is something peculiar. They are taught that China is the center of the earth, and that the people who live around the edges of that blissful country are wild to get into it. They learn that some of these outside barbarians hop on one leg, that others have claws like a bird; some, they are told, have one eye in their foreheads, and others have holes through their bodies, so that they can be carried by a pole thrust through. To which of these races we belong they haven't told us yet.

There's one very lovely thing about the Chinese, which will be pleasant to hear, after all these unpleasant things. They are fond of pets, and are very kind to them. Birds of various kinds are kept as pets, and it is not at all uncommon to see fine-looking, elegantly dressed gentlemen taking their birds out for an airing, either in a cage, or perched on their finger. They catch insects to feed them, and even take them to the mountains for change of air.

Crows are not hated, but are taught cunning tricks and winning ways, and pigeons have bamboo whistles fastened to their feathers, so they make noise as they fly. Even cats are taught to live in bird-houses, to protect the birds from rats.

One very popular bird pet is called, at least by travelers, the tumbler, because his constant delight is to turn somersets on his perch. Over and over, again and again, this queer fellow will go, every time alighting on his feet, and appearing to do it purely for fun.

Perhaps the queerest pet (and of course the Chinese would have something of that sort) is the cricket. This little creature belongs more to the boys perhaps, though many grown-up men and women keep them. They are carefully fed, and provided with water, in pretty little bamboo cages, and often carried out with the owner. The ladies like them for their cheerful chirps, but the men and boys match them for fighting.

It must be great sport to see a cricket fight in a tub! The insect which beats in several fights is regarded with honor, has a special name, and is buried in a silver coffin.

A Chinese story is somewhat different from those you have heard before. It is very often about boys who have risen from poverty to be great men by study, for much as we may laugh at what we consider their queer ways, we must acknowledge that the people of China have a sincere respect for intelligence and learning.

And we must not forget, either, that our ways are as strange to them, and they do not hesitate to laugh at us, to make fun of us, by pictures and in other ways.

The story I will tell you is as well known to the Chinese boy, says Mr. Williams (from whose book I take it), as the story of Washington and his hatchet is to you. It is about one of those very, very good, and dreadfully wise boys, that one rarely sees outside of the story-books. It is about

Confucius and Hiang Toh.

"The name of Confucius was Yu, and his style Chungni; he established himself as an instructor in the western part of the kingdom of Lu. One day, followed by all his disciples, riding in a carriage, he went out to ramble, and on the road came across several children at their sports; among them was one who did not join in them. Confucius, stopping his carriage, asked him, saying:

"'Why is it that you alone do not play?'

"The lad replied:

"'All play is without any profit; one's clothes get torn and they are not easily mended; above me I disgrace my father, and mother; below me there is fighting and altercation; so much toil and no reward, how can it be a good business? It is for these reasons that I do not play.'

"Then dropping his head he began making a city out of pieces of tile. Confucius reproving him, said:

"'Why do you not turn out for the carriage?'

"The boy replied:

"'From ancient times until now, it has always been considered proper for a carriage to turn out for a city, and not for a city to turn out for a carriage.'

"Confucius then stopped his vehicle in order to discourse of reason. He got out of the carriage and asked him:

"'You are still young in years, how is it that you are so quick?'

"The boy replied, saying:

"'A human being at the age of three years discriminates between his father and mother; a hare, three days after it is born, runs over the ground; fish, three days after their birth, wander in rivers and lakes; what heaven thus produces naturally, how can it be called brisk?'

"Confucius added:

"'In what village and neighborhood do you reside; what is your surname and name, and what your style?'

"The boy answered:

"'I live in a mean village, and in an insignificant land; my surname is Hiang, my name is Toh, and I have yet no style.'

"Confucius rejoined:

"'I wish to have you come and ramble with me; what do you think of it?'

"The youth replied:

"'A stern father is at home, whom I am bound to serve; an affectionate mother is there, whom it is my duty to cherish; a worthy elder brother is at home whom it is proper for me to obey, with a tender younger brother whom I must teach; and an intelligent teacher is there, from whom I am required to learn. How have I leisure to go a-rambling with you?'

"Confucius said:

"'I have in my carriage thirty-two chessmen; what do you say to having a game together?'

"The lad answered:

"'If the emperor love gaming, the empire will not be governed; if the nobles love play, the government will be impeded; if scholars love it, learning and investigation will be lost and thrown by; if the lower classes are fond of gambling they will utterly lose the support of their families; if servants and slaves love to game, they will get a cudgeling; if farmers love it, they miss the time for ploughing and sowing; for these reasons I shall not play with you.'

[I shall have to omit some of this long story, for I'm sure you would skip the wise replies of this little phenomenon. After a while Confucius put some conundrums to him.]

"'Can you tell under the whole sky what fire has no smoke, what water no fish; what man has no wife, what woman no husband; what constitutes an excellent man, and what an inferior man; what is that which has not enough, and what that which has an overplus; what city is without a market; and who is the man without a style?'

"The boy replied:

"'A glow-worm's fire has no smoke, and well-water no fish; genii have no wives, and fairies no husbands; he who is worthy is an excellent man, and a fool is an inferior man; a winter's day is not long enough, and a summer's day is too long; the imperial city has no market, and little folks have no style.'

[After several more questions, and equally wise answers, the boy takes his turn at asking.]

"'Why is it that mallards and ducks are able to swim; how is it that wild geese and cranes sing; and why are firs and pines green through the winter?'

"Confucius replied:

"'Mallards and ducks can swim because their feet are broad; wild geese and cranes can sing because they have long necks;

firs and pines remain green through the winter because they have strong hearts.'

"The youth rejoined:

"'Not so; fishes and turtles can swim, is it because they all have broad feet? frogs and toads can sing, is it because their necks are long? the green bamboo keeps fresh in winter, is it on account of its strong heart?'

"Again interrogating, he said:

"'How many stars are there all together in the sky?'

"Confucius replied:

"'At this time inquire about the earth; how can we converse about the sky with certainty?'

"The boy said:

"'Then how many houses in all are there upon the earth?'

"The sage answered:

"'Come now, speak about something that is before our eyes; why must you converse about heaven and earth?'

"The lad resumed:

"'Well, speak about what's before our eyes; how many hairs are there in your eyebrows?'

"Confucius smiled, but did not answer, and turning round to his disciples, called them, and said:

"'This boy is to be feared; for it is easy to see that the subsequent man will not be like the child.'

"He then got into his carriage and rode off."

There's another sort of story quite as popular as these about preternatually wise boys who are able to put their teachers to shame, or boys and girls so very, very good that they quite overwhelm their relatives and friends. They deal with magic. Here is a little one (from Mr. Williams's book also). We will call it

The Magic Plum-tree.

" A villager was once selling plums in the market, which were rather delicious and fragrant, and high in price; and there was a Tau priest, clad in ragged garments of coarse cotton, begging before his wagon.

" The villager scolded him, but he would not go off; whereupon, becoming angry, he reviled and hooted at him. The priest said:

" 'The wagon contains many hundred plums, and I have only begged one of them, which for you, respected sir, would certainly be no great loss; why, then, are you so angry?'

" The spectators advised to give him a poor plum and send him away, but the villager would not consent.

" The workmen in the market, disliking the noise and clamor, furnished a few coppers, and bought a plum, which they gave the priest. He, bowing, thanked them, and turning to the crowd, said:

" 'I do not wish to be stingy, and request you, my friends, to partake with me of this delicious plum.'

" One of them replied:

" 'Now you have it, why do you not eat it yourself?'

" 'I want only the stone to plant!' said he, eating it up at a munch.

" When eaten, he held the stone in his hand, and taking a spade off his shoulder, dug a hole in the ground several inches deep, into which he put it, and covered it with earth.

" Then turning to the market-people, he procured some broth, with which he watered and fertilized it; and others, wishing to see what would turn up, brought him boiling dregs from shops near by, which he poured upon the hole just dug.

"Every one's eyes being fixed upon the spot, they saw a crooked shoot issuing forth, which gradually increased till it became a tree, having branches and leaves; flowers, and then fruit succeeded, large, and very fragrant, which covered the tree.

"The priest approached the tree, plucked the fruit and gave the beholders; and when all were consumed, he felled the tree with a colter, chopping, chopping for a good while, until at last, having cut it off, he shouldered the foliage in an easy manner and leisurely walked away.

"When first the priest began to perform his magic arts, the villager was also among the crowd, with outstretched neck and gazing eyes, and completely forgot his own business. When the priest had gone he began to look into his own wagon, and lo! it was empty of plums; and for the first time he perceived that what had just been distributed were all his own goods.

"Moreover, looking narrowly about his wagon he saw that the dashboard was gone, having just been cut off with a chisel. Much excited and incensed, he ran after him, and as he turned the corner of the wall, he saw the board thrown down beneath the hedge, it being that with which the plum-tree was felled. Nobody knew where the priest had gone, and all the market-folks laughed heartily."

CHAPTER XIV.

THE HAPPIEST BABY OF ALL; THE LITTLE JAPANESE.

I HAVE saved till the last the youngster that has the very happiest time of any little body in the world.

Not because I didn't wish to tell about him. No, indeed! All the time you were hearing about the unfortunate little Turk, the naughty little Syrian, the caste-bound little Hindu, and worst of all, the wretched little Chinese, I kept thinking of this dear comfortable little soul, and longing to tell.

But I thought I would keep the best for the last, and so here it is, the happiest of all, the baby of Japan.

A queer, wise-looking little bundle is the Japanese Ko; a baby without a cradle or baby-carriage, who never cries, and is never kissed, and who looks exactly like a picture from a fan or a teapot. Here he is, on his nurse's back.

This little man, who looks so solemn that one wouldn't venture to address him in what is called "baby talk," begins his life, according to law, with twenty-four dresses, twelve of silk, and twelve of cotton, with the hems dyed yellow.

It seems rather droll for the law to dictate how many dresses a baby shall have, but the Japanese wise men go even beyond this in their laws. One of baby's dresses must be made from his mother's girdle, which has been dyed sky-blue, and after the child's first bath it must be dried with a cotton kerchief without a hem.

These important matters being properly attended to, the baby gets a name when he is seven days old. Getting a name is not for life, as it is for you; it is only for his first seven years. At seven he has a new name, and at fifteen still another. He's even more changeable in the matter of names than a Chinese, for all through life, when he goes to a new place, begins a new business, or goes out of business altogether, he takes a new one. It is, of course, his given name which is so often changed.

THE JAPANESE KO.

"Never cries," I said, and so say the people who have visited him in his home. Now, this is the second baby we have found in Asia, who never, or almost never, indulges in the terrible shrieks that nearly drive us frantic in our nurseries. The reason is the same in both cases, *they are comfortable!*

The little Hindu is quiet and calm, because he has not a rag to bind him anywhere, not a pin to prick, nor a string to cut; and the little Japanese, though warmly dressed, is equally happy. His dress is loose and soft, he rolls about on the clean mats of the floor, with no tables or chairs to hurt himself against, no stairs to fall down, no stove to burn him. He has no curls to be combed, and no shoes to pinch him; no "don't touch" rings in his ears, and a slap is a thing unknown. He can't get into mischief in a Japanese house, and so he is never scolded. Now, why shouldn't a baby be happy and good-natured in Japan?

There's another reason; his father and mother take life easier than we do. They never grow so very much older than the little folks, that they forget the time they were young themselves. They play with them, and in every way enter into their lives. When the mothers go out to visit their friends, the little folks go too, as you see in this happy picture, where everybody, from the droll little baby on mamma's back to the great lady with the parasol, seems to be having a good time. The little people are not the only happy ones in Japan.

While the Japanese Ko is still young he is labelled (as it were), so that he shall not be lost. The name and address of his parents is engraved upon a brass plate, which is always fastened to his girdle. If he loses his way, the first older person who sees him can easily learn where he belongs, and return him to his home.

Because this child has no baby carriage, do not fancy he stays at home. He sees much more of the life about him than do our poor little bundled-up babies, covered with a veil, and laid flat on their backs, where they can see only the sky, generally with a glaring sun in it, or the parasol which shades them.

The poor baby of Japan sees the world from the back of somebody. Sometimes it is mamma who carries him about at her work, or in her walks: but oftener it is an older brother or sister. Perhaps the elder may be scarcely able to toddle about

GOING TO MAKE A CALL.

himself, yet baby is strapped to his back, and he goes out to run around the streets, to play and jump, as if he had no burden at all.

He gets many a tumble, and his head joggles about as though it would come off; but he doesn't mind that; he looks as wise as an owl, with his little bare head so close to his brother's or sister's, that they together look like a two-headed monster of some sort.

AN ARISTOCRATIC BABY.

The rich, or at least the aristocratic youngster of Japan, has a nurse, or an officer to carry him about. Now the upper classes, even the babies, have a right to carry two swords, so this grave little fellow will have, perhaps, a short sword in his own girdle, while a large one is carried for him by the nurse, or by another attendant. Soon after he can stand on his own feet, however, he wears his own two swords. Here is a picture of one of these little fellows, led by his servant, with his sister carrying his sword.

[I ought, perhaps, to say he used to do so, for great changes are going on in Japan, and things are different now. But, as I have said before, I want to tell you of the *native* manners, not of those which are copied from other people.]

All this time the youngster's head has been shaved clean as a base-ball (a new one, by the way), but he grows very fast out of babyhood. First, he learns, not to creep, like our babies, but to squat! and to sit on his heels! This is the Japanese way, and this he must learn. When he has lived a certain number of days, not far from four months, he goes through a formal ceremony of taking solid food, and putting off baby-clothes.

The food is rice, and it is to be hoped that he likes it, for rice he will eat every day of his life, if he lives to be a hundred years old. If the child is a boy, he is fed on this important occasion by a gentleman, if it is a girl she is fed by a lady.

As soon as the little one can stand, begins his training in "manners" Ah! now, American little folk, hide your heads with shame, while I tell you what all travelers agree in saying about these little men and women far over the sea, whom we laugh at, and think so inferior to ourselves. Listen!

In the matter of behavior the child of Japan is perfection; almost its first words are "please" and "thank you;" before he can walk well he can fall on his knees and bow his head to the ground, which he does every morning to father and mother, and by the time he is ten years old, he is as perfect in the forms of politeness as his parents themselves. He is gentle and obedient, he is ready to help; no cross "I don't want to" comes when he is asked to do anything. He is good to smaller children, he does not "bully" nor abuse them.

And, oh, dear children, listen to what one observing traveler says of these little men and women. "In all Japan I never heard an angry word, or saw a sour look."

If one does chance to forget for a moment his "manners," he is severely punished in some way (not by whipping) and the offense promptly apologized for. One case is told where a child called a traveler "Foreign Devil" a common thing to be heard in China, and about as if you should call a Chinaman "Heathen Chinee." The child was reproved at once, and a policeman sent to the lady to make an apology for his ill manners.

The grave dignity of these little people is funny to see, and their dress makes them look like old people cut down. But don't think for a moment that the little Japanese are "prigs," or that they don't have splendid times. Nowhere on the round globe do they have more fun than in Japan. In fact the country has been called "The Paradise of Children;" though they do not enjoy the rough-and-tumble games you like, the pulling and pushing, the scrambling, the shrieking, and the angry words.

They consider such things barbarous, and would no more do them than would your father and mother. They do wrestle together, and growl at each other like two dogs in unhappy mood, just as the grown-up wrestlers do, but they do not get angry over it, nor do they have such a rough time as you do in wrestling.

To speak again of the baby; at four years old thin patches of hair are allowed to grow on his head, one on the back and one on each side, as you have seen in Japanese dolls; and at five years the upper-class youngster is put into the very wide trowsers worn by his rank.

SITTING BY THE FIRE.

As to the dress of little people, it is exactly like that of the grown-ups, and is simply a dressing-gown tied around the waist with a girdle. This is—or was till lately—almost the only dress of the common people of Japan, from the baby of two, to the grandfather and grandmother, men, women, and children all alike.

When the weather is warm, they wear one thin garment of this shape folded over in front and held in place by a belt; if it is cold, they add more of the same shape, thickly wadded, and made of silk or cotton according to the length of their purse.

Men and big boys wear belts three or four inches wide, but women and girls have sashes a foot or more wide and tied in an immense bow at the back, often with stiffening in to keep them in shape.

There are no underclothes to drag on one, no hats to look after, no shoes to pinch one's toes. Think how nice and easy one would feel! Dress up in papa's dressing-gown some day, tie it loosely around the waist, put on a pair of stockings, and see how comfortable you'll be. Then remember, you girls, that there are no ruffles and neckties, no ruches, no collars, no ribbons, no French heels and no tight waists, truly not a restraint upon one anywhere; what luxury!

See them on the page back sitting by the fire, waiting for the tea-kettle to boil.

I don't say I admire everything about the Japanese dress, but I do say it is comfortable.

By way of ornament to the dressing-gown, boys often have the crest of their family embroidered on the back.

The Japanese youngster's stocking is a funny affair. It is to take the place of both stocking and slipper in the house, for the high clogs and sandals he wears in the street, are always left at the door when he goes in. His stockings, therefore, are made of cloth, not woven or knit like ours. They are white or some color, with very thick soles, and shaped like a mitten, with a separate place for the big toe. This fashion is not to do honor to the big toe, but to make a place through which may go the straps of the clogs, since they are held on by one strap alone.

Perhaps you are shocked at the idea of going about the house in white stockings, and in our houses it would not be very nice. But a house in Japan is quite a different affair.

A Japanese house is like a doll-house, and neat as a pin from roof to floor. It is small and low, and looks as if made for a family of wax dolls. The only really solid things about most of these houses are the roof, which is of wood, and the floor. The side walls (always on two sides, and often on all four) are of paper, stretched upon frames, and make to slide back. A thinner paper stretched over a lattice-work screen is the only apology for a window.

Isn't this like a box? Think of a house without doors or windows! If you want to go out you simply shove one side a part of the wall of the house, and walk out anywhere. On the next page is a lady in her room, made by screens.

This is not very secure against thieves! That is true; but nearly every house has behind it a small fireproof building, of a more solid kind, in which are kept all the treasures of the family. Their valuable old china, their beautiful wall pictures, in fact, all valuables are locked up in this storehouse.

We shouldn't think pictures were of much use locked up in a storehouse, but that's another thing in which the Japanese differ from us. They do not show all their pretty things at once. For a few days one picture will hang on the wall to be looked at and admired, and then it will be taken away and another one brought out. So you see they have variety all the time.

The want of doors and windows is not the only queer thing about the little Jap's home. There's not a chair in the house, nor a bedstead, nor even a bed; not a table, except one fit for

SCREENS FOR WALLS.

dolls, about six inches high, as you see in the picture of Japanese girls. Not a fork, not a table-cloth, nor a sheet.

All the family cooking is done within its paper walls; yet

there is not a stove, nor fire-place, nor even a chimney to the house. Outside the door hangs a list of the names of the people inside, and if a guest comes his name must be added at once. Drollest of all, to prevent the rat family from cutting doors through the walls, in the irregular shape that rats usually cut them, the builders kindly cut square doors for the small gnawers to come in!

Have you guessed the conundrum about the cooking? How can they cook without a stove? How can they make smoke without a chimney? They cook over a small brass dish of coals, which is placed on a box of sand, so as not to set the house afire (as you saw in the picture); and they have no smoke because they use charcoal.

Dinner looks like a "make believe" dolls' party. It is served in tiny bowls the size of tea-cups, on a six-inch-high table, that may be a foot and a half square; just a fair doll's table. Tea is drunk from cups as big as a thimble, and the diners sit on the floor to eat. It's a real doll-house affair, altogether.

But I said no chairs? Now you see why everybody sits on the floor! Another thing about it, there's no lounging in all Japan; one must lie down or sit up, for there are not only no easy chairs, but not even solid walls to lean against. If one leaned against a wall he would break through to the outside.

The whole house is one room, with paper walls, and thick, soft, white mats on the floor; but if rooms are wanted they are easily made in this paper play-house. Screens of paper on frames are slid into grooves between the mats of the floor, and a room partitioned off in a few minutes. To be sure, there is no privacy about it; one can hear every word spoken in the house, and a pin-hole through the wall is as good as a window to "peek" through.

There is, of course, no such thing as locking one's door, and going to bed is as simple as it is, to us, odd. To begin with, everybody takes a hot bath, and puts on his day clothes again. Then the house is shut up, all screens slid into their places, leaving not a crack for fresh air, and beds are made.

This is as much like doll's doings as the rest; a thick quilt is spread on the mat of the floor; over one's day clothes is put a long wadded wrapper with enormous sleeves. Next, a pillow of wood, shaped like a cradle-rocker, and having a wad of paper to rest the neck on, is placed at the head, which, by the way, must not be towards the north. So particular are the people about the points of the compass, that private houses have them marked on the walls, and many carry a small compass with them, that no mistake shall be made.

This matter settled, the one going to bed places at his (or her) head a tray of food, and smoking utensils, lest he (or she) should wake in the night and wish to eat or smoke. A lantern, too, belongs to the sleeping-room; for one and all, from grandpa down to the least Japanese ko, dislike darkness, and always keep lights burning at night.

On his quilt the contented Japanese, in his big night-wrapper, lies down, draws over him another quilt, lays his neck across his wooden rocker, and goes to sleep. All our fuss of bedstead and beds, sheets, blankets, and pillow-cases, are to him unnecessary. See how comfortable he looks in the picture all settled for the night.

You see he doesn't need a big house; a doll-house will do for him. He can eat anywhere, cook anywhere, and sleep anywhere. He needs neither kitchen, dining-room, nor bed-room.

In the morning he gets up, shakes himself out, rolls quilts, bed-robe, and pillow into a package, which he shuts up in a cup-board, slides back the screens from the front of the house, dusts off the matting, and the Japanese house is in perfect order for the day.

Think of our morning work—the sweeping and dusting, bed

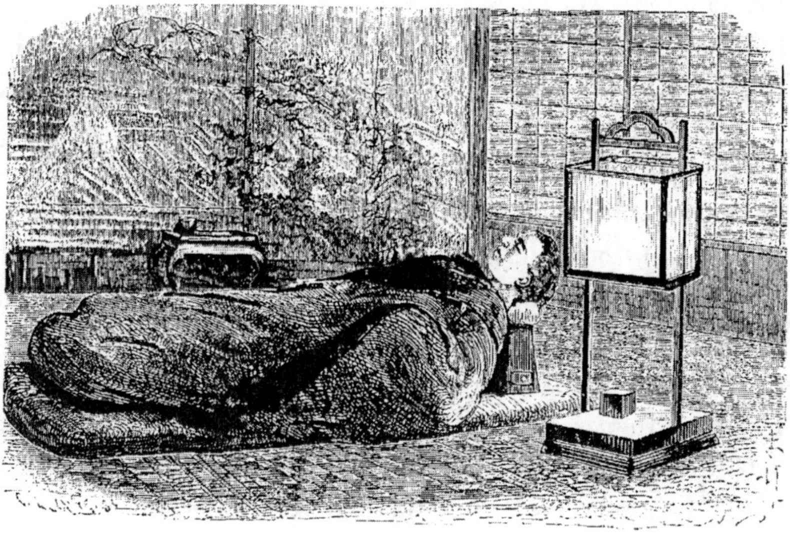

ABED AND ASLEEP.

making, and putting in order! Japan is a paradise for house-keepers as well as for babies.

The baby Jap does exactly what his father does. He has no nursery; he is always with his parents; he learns their talk; he gets up and goes to bed when they do; with them he goes to the public baths, or joins the group of bathers in steaming hot water at evening in the house.

This same Japanese baby is a droll-looking object, exactly

like the big dolls our merchants bring from there. They are so much like them that travelers say they have often mistaken a doll on the back of its little mistress for a baby, especially as most of the little girls in the street are saddled with the baby.

The dolls, you know, have little hair, a tuft like the end of a brush on top, and perhaps another over each ear. That is a perfect copy of the head of the real live baby. His head is kept shaved, except these spots, till grown up, and even then most of the hair and all of the beard is shaved off.

Soon after a boy is fifteen a lucky day is chosen, on which the forelock is cut off and he is considered a man, and of age (as we say). There is a great feast given in the family, and rejoicing on all sides.

The hair of Japanese girls is allowed to grow, and is worn in "bangs" in front, and done up behind in different styles according to her age and condition. The way a girl's or woman's hair is done up tells to every one who sees it whether she is married or single, whether she is a widow, and even whether she would be willing to marry again or not.

Girls learn to sew, in this happy land, but fine stitches do not bother her. She has to make nothing more than the one-shaped garment of Japan, and that is simply basted together, so that it may be easily taken apart for washing.

There are no handkerchiefs to hem; Japanese handkerchiefs are of soft paper, and thrown away when once used. The only undergarments of Japan are worn by the upper class, and are made of soft silk crape, in the same dressing-gown shape.

Girls embroider, but that is not work, and they are taught to arrange flowers. They make more of this than we do, and consequently do it in much better taste than we. No stiff, dreadful bunches, where all sorts are jammed in together, are ever seen in Japan, like those that are common with us, but one sort alone, even one spray in a vase by itself with its own leaves and branches. Books are written on the subject of arranging flowers in Japan, and it might be well for us to have some translations.

Little girls dress like their mothers, as I said, even the little ones as you see them here, only the colors are gayer; scarlet flowered brocade for the wide sash, and scarlet crape in the hair They have also pretty embroidered cases stuck in the belt, to hold a quire of pocket handkerchiefs—think of carrying a quire of handkerchiefs!

THEY DRESS LIKE MAMMA.

The belt is in fact the most useful part of a Japanese dress. From it hang the purse, the school-books, done up in a square piece of silk, the half-round embroidered pocket of the school boy, the scarlet embroidered pocket of the girl, and the oversash of the same color which is to keep the big sash knot in place; the ink and pen, and smoking apparatus of the father, the handkerchiefs and other things of the mother. In it too is always stuck the fan.

But the pocket proper is the queerest thing. Where would

you guess a pocket would be? Never, I'm sure, could you guess. It is in the sleeve! The sleeves are made of a straight piece of the cloth, folded and sewed together, and are often long enough to touch the ground. Only a little of this width is needed as a sleeve, and the rest is sewed up in front to make a sort of bag or pocket, into which are put the choicest treasures of the wearer.

These enormous sleeves are often a nuisance, In boys' play they are apt to trail and get wet; and servant girls (who wear the same sort, of course) have an arrangement of braces to hold them back out of the way, while they work.

Now hear about the school; we've seen some queer schools in our travels about the world, and the Japanese one has its odd points. It begins—oh dear!—at seven o'clock in the morning! before many little Americans have their eyes open. But it doesn't last till four o'clock; it ends at twelve, and that's all for that day.

Bad scholars are punished, of course; they have to be punished, I find, all over the world. Even the very, very good little Jap is not always perfect, and the teacher is obliged to—to—*burn him!*

No whipping! no marking! no "keeping in!" but a neat little "moxa" on his finger. This "moxa" is a favorite punishment at home too, and it is also used as a cure by the doctors. It is simply a little cone-shaped bit of some sort of pith, which burns slowly, like the punk you light your fire-crackers with. It is put on the finger of a naughty scholar, lighted, and let burn as long as the teacher thinks he deserves. Here is the school, and some of the boys'll get the moxa if they don't stop teasing the cat. (See frontispiece.)

At twelve o'clock the little people are dismissed, go home to dinner, and after that they play; and the games and the toys of Japan are endless.

First there's the doll, and the doll is first in Japan, I assure you. Even the mothers do not disdain to play with dolls to please their children. The dolls themselves are of all sizes and kinds; those that walk, that dance, and that put on a mask; they are taken to walk, dressed and undressed, put to bed, and taken out "to tea;" they have their own tea-sets and bedding, and their own houses; they play sick, and in fact mimic the life around them, as do dolls and their mistresses all over the world.

The great time of the year for the little Japanese girl comes on the third day of March. For some time before this day the shops are full of dolls and girls' playthings; not a thing of the boyish sort will be seen. Fathers and mothers go out to buy dolls and dolls' furniture, toilet sets, wardrobes, and dozens of other things.

On the evening before the great day, the feast of dolls; after the little people are in bed, the fire-proof room of the house is opened, and dolls by the dozen, yes, by the hundred, are brought out, each wrapped carefully in silk paper. Tables are prepared, and the dolls ("Hina," the girls call them) set out, with their furniture and toys, with flowers and cakes. Some of these dolls have come down from the little girl's grandmother, and great-grandmother, for it is the custom in Japan to buy a pair of dolls as soon as a girl baby arrives, let her play with them till she is married, and then take them to her own house.

On the great day they are brought out, with the pairs that belonged to her ancestors also. They are made of wood, or enameled clay, and gorgeously dressed to represent different characters in history; the mikado and his wife, and mythological characters. Their dresses do not get out of fashion, for fashions do not (or did not) change in that country. Some of the dolls are four feet high.

The special dolls of the little girls, I mean those they play with every day, are as much loved as are yours. As I told you above, they are treated as *if* they were babies, have their wadded bed-gown, and pair of silk or muslin quilts; they have their toy wooden pillows, and sleep, like their little mistress, under green mosquito curtains. They take their meals on a table four inches square.

JAPANESE PICTURE OF A HERO.

Besides the doll and its belongings, Japanese girls play battledore and shuttlecock, and many other games, as well as enjoy toy and story books, of which they have great quantities, of the Mother Goose sort.

For the baby boy is bought a banner stand, which holds the banners of generals and military heroes. He must have a toy helmet, to remind him that he must some day be a soldier. He has a sort of doll, too—figures of famous men and heroes, perhaps like that on the last page, which was drawn by a Japanese, and is in great favor.

THE BABY'S BANNER STAND.

Here is a baby boy's first banner stand, with its curious banners, and the baby himself enjoying it. This too is a Japanese picture.

The boys' great day is on the fifth of May, and at that time the girls' toys have disappeared from the shops, and only boys' things are to be bought. Before every house where there are boys, a tall pole is planted, and from the top of it floats a big fish, sometimes twenty feet long, made of paper so as to be light, and having its mouth held open by a hoop, so that the air will fill it.

The shops display warlike figures, toy animals, tents, racks for arms, and such things. Then there are the full equipments for a procession of one of the grandees of Japan, as it used to be in the old times. The boys play this procession, with its officers, and men running on before to clear the way.

They play also at a sham battle, when every boy has a flag, and the object of every other boy is to snatch it away. The boy who loses his flag must go out of the game; or they have the flag fastened on the back, and on the head a flat, round piece of earthenware. Each boy in this game has a bamboo sword, and tries to break the earthenware on his neighbor's head. If he succeeds, the owner of the broken ware has to leave, as if his skull was broken.

The boys play whip-top, blind-man's-buff (called "eye-hiding"), puss-in-the-corner, knuckle-bones, or jack-stones, with stuffed bags for stones. They hide the slipper, or, rather, the shoe, have pop-guns, walk on stilts, and run as well, and play games on them. In the snow they coast and slide, make forts, play battle, and make a snow man, not a common-looking creature smoking a pipe, but a figure of Daruma, a follower of Buddha, their great prophet, who meditated so long in one position that he lost his legs, and is always represented without any. This is an easy figure, you see, for the legs of a snow man are the hardest to make nicely.

In the evening, at home, the family gather around the fire-box, as we do around a fire, father, mother, and all, and tell stories, or play games of proverbs or puzzles, called "wisdom-boards," or backgammon, or chess, or make shadow pictures on the walls.

ANOTHER DANCER.

Amusements are without end for the little Japanese. He can hardly go into the street without seeing a strolling show of some sort—plays, peep-shows, posturers, dancers, like this elegant creature; singers, toy-peddlers, or boy acrobats, who stand on their hands, and bring their feet over till they rest on their own head, and many other marvelous things. And above all other street pleasures, the batter-cake-man, who has batter and hot griddle always ready, and for a very small coin allows a child to cook cakes for himself, in any shape he pleases. What fun!

Then the youngsters are taken to the theatre, which opens in the morning, and runs one play all day. Families go together, take their lunch, and the little bowl of ashes and hot coals to make their tea, and stay till night. The play is often a fairy story, as a tea-pot that turned into a badger, called "The Bubbling Tea-pot," and others of a similar kind. Here is a restaurant of a theatre, with all its queer sights, eating, and drinking, and music.

Or the show may be a performance with false noses, like the picture farther on, where everything is done with those members, even to writing on the wall.

Then there are dances to be seen, which are very different from ours—a fan dance, a shuttlecock dance, ball dances, and umbrella dances, which are both curious and amusing. In the picture you see one of these odd dances. It is the "Butterfly Dance." The dancers are dressed to imitate butterflies, and you can see by the one whose back is turned how good the imitation is. You can see there also the dress of the great ladies of Japan.

There are other queer costumes of actors; one like a bird, another like a cock, and others like—dear me! what *are* they like? Can you tell?

Besides these a religious dance, and a beggars' dance.

But the fireworks are the greatest show. They are of two sorts, for day as well as for night. The evening fireworks are not so very different from ours, but those displayed in the day-

BETWEEN THE ACTS.

light are unlike anything we have seen, until, within the last year, some few have been shown by Japanese themselves, near New York city.

THE BUTTERFLY DANCE.

These daylight fireworks are shot out of a bamboo mortar, and go far up in the air like a ball, and then burst with a loud explosion. Sometimes there fall a great number of Japanese

WITH FALSE NOSES.

parasols of doll size, sometimes flags by the hundred; but the most interesting are figures of men and animals. These figures unfold, and sail off in the air, life-size, or larger, and very curious they are, too. There may be an old woman hobbling along on

ACTORS

a cane, or an old man smoking a pipe, out of which, as he sails away in the sky, comes a fox. There may be a very-much-scared mouse with a cat after it, a monkey blowing soap-bubbles, and others both hideous and funny.

The figures are colored like life, and it looks very queer to see them sailing away on the breeze, always right side up, and at last, perhaps, falling into the sea, and floating awhile before they sink. They are made of paper, or light silk, and have tiny lead weights to keep them right side up, and holes to let the air in to float them.

A RELIGIOUS DANCE.

No people in the world are so fond of the funny and the grotesque as the Japanese. They even grow their shrubs and plants in queer shapes. This is done by means of bamboo frames, of the shape they wish; it may be a cockatoo ten feet high, a Chinese junk, or an English lady. On this frame they train the plant, and make the blossoms come in such a way as to color the figures as they like. I mean, for instance, to make the lady's dress of white flowers, with another color to trim it.

They make things grow about as they choose; trees an inch or two high, or cherry-blossoms double, and as big as a rose.

I haven't spoken of kites, though they are almost as popular in Japan as in China. They are not of so many shapes; in

THE BEGGARS' DANCE

fact, they are more often square than otherwise, but the people seem to enjoy them quite as much as the Chinese. The game with these toys is to cut the string of another kite, and for this purpose the string is covered with powdered glass. When one boy cuts the string of another boy's kite, the fallen one belongs

LANTERN PEDDLER.

to him. There is no quarrel about it, nor does the loser go off mad; he gives up his kite with three low bows.

Ah, how charming! Aren't you ashamed of your rude ways, when you think of the elegant manners of your little neighbors over the sea?

A kite-shop has a funny sign—nothing less than a cuttle-fish, because the word for kite, "tako," means, likewise, cuttle-fish.

Japanese boys send messengers up to their kites, as you do, only much prettier than yours, for when it nearly reaches the kite, a little jerk of the string opens the small bundle, and down falls a shower of red and white bits of paper, like a snow-storm. Sometimes, too, their kites are musical, having a bit of thin whalebone which vibrates in the air, and makes a humming sound.

The boys are so fond of big kites, that they would have them as big as the side of a house, only it is not allowed by law. The reason a law of this sort was made is, because at one time a party of thieves stole some of the gold scales off a fish which ornamented the top of a castle, and got at it by help of an enormous kite, big enough to carry up a man. The kite-cord was held by a windlass, and the man had his feet in loops on the kite tail, and was safely flown over the castle, alighted where he wished, and stole the gold.

In almost every picture of Japan we see lanterns, and they are as common in real life as on the fans and other things that come to us, and lantern peddlers are seen everywhere Everybody carries one at night, and nearly every house has one hanging outside. Should it rain, an umbrella is hung over them. Fancy our lamp-posts with umbrellas over them!

One thing the little Japanese is never without is the fan;

indeed, everybody, from the king on his throne to the porter that carries loads in the street, carries a fan. The teacher uses it for a ruler, the cook to fan his fire, the farmer carries it into the fields, and the juggler flaunts it from the top of his pile.

A FAMOUS HERO.

They are of waterproof paper for the wet, strong to winnow grain, and gay-colored for the dancing girls

Even the famous old warriors make use of the fan, as you see in this picture of a very celebrated Japanese character, whose plan was to flirt his fan in the face of his enemy, to distract his attention, and then to give him a sudden thrust with his savage-looking sword. This great personage is what horsemen would call a "free stepper," isn't he?

In every house is a silver rack, or some sort of a fan-holder. They are used for autographs, for maps, or for useful information.

What does our little Japanese eat? He has no bread or butter, no milk or coffee, no puddings, pies, or custards. If his father is not rich, he eats little meat except fish, but principally rice and vegetables cooked into queer-looking messes (to us), served in little bowls, and eaten with chop-sticks. Fruits he is fond of, cucumbers he delights in (even the babies suck them), and persimmons are large size and a golden color. Beans he eats covered with sugar like a sugared almond, or made into jelly, which must be droll to see.

You would like to go to a Japanese girl's party, I know; but the best I can do is to tell you about one that took place in a house where an English lady, Miss Bird, was staying, and which she tells about in her delightful book.

It was a formal party given by a girl of twelve. The guests came at about three o'clock in the afternoon, and the girl, named Haru, received them at the top of the steps, and invited them into the house, arranging them according to their rank in the most proper way.

Haru's dress was elegant. Her hair was drawn back, raised in front, and made into a big double loop, with scarlet crape twisted in it. Her face and throat were thick with a white sort of paint, which came to an end in the back of her neck, in three points, considered very stylish indeed. Her lips were painted red, and she looked exactly like a cheap doll.

Her dress was of blue flowered silk, with sleeves that touched the ground, a blue sash lined with scarlet, and a fold of scarlet in her neck (instead of a ruche). On her feet she had white stockings, with elegant lacquered clogs for outside. In her hair were hair-pins, representing a tiny gold battledore, with coral shuttlecock.

Her guests were dressed in the same style, and looked like a party of big dolls. Haru met them with very formal bows, and when they were seated about the floor, she went around and, squatting before each one, offered her tea and sweetmeats, among which, I suppose, were sugared beans.

After this they played very quiet and polite games, addressing each other with the honorable prefix O, and the respectful addition of San, as, for instance, Haru was O-Haru-San. As if you should call your friend "Miss." They could do no more by Haru's mother; they called her O-Kami-San.

One game they played was amusing, though done with the greatest dignity. It was playing "sick," as you've done a hundred times. One was the invalid, and another the doctor, and both played their parts very well. The patient died, and they played bury her, and go into mourning and all.

When it grew dark, and was time to go home, the dignified little misses were served again with tea and sweetmeats, and according to the rules of Japanese etiquette, none must be left. So when one had eaten all she wished, she slipped the remainder into her sleeve.

Then came the formal bows and good-byes, and the guests went home. It was exceedingly funny; a picture of big folks' life by little folks.

In Japan, as well as in China, many things are exactly the

wrong way, in our opinion. Shoes are made by a carpenter, cows' bells are hung to their tails, horses' tails are put into silk bags and tied up with silk tassels, and they wear straw shoes that are tied up with shoestrings. In the stable, horses' heads

PAINTING UPSIDE DOWN.

are where their tails should be; the meat-safe hangs from the kitchen wall like a bird-cage, and the candle is hollow, and is stuck on a spike.

Lambs are emblems of obstinacy, and to call one a goose is a compliment. To drive away a dog they say "Choo," and to please a person they call him old.

Workmen sit down to work; artists sometimes paint upside down, screws turn the wrong way, and toys squeak when pulled. Grown-ups ride in baby carriages drawn by a man, and dogs wear ruffles on their necks.

In building a house, the roof is made first, and hoisted into

AN ORNAMENTED ROOF.

place, and see what a funny roof they will make of it on a festive occasion; and to injure an enemy, a Japanese kills, not the enemy, but himself!

There are no sidewalks in Jeddo; turn over the leaf and see how the streets look; there are no Sundays, and no jewelry from one end of Japan to the other.

To get rid of a bore they go into the kitchen, turn the broom upside down, and fan it (!), and to do honor to one of their gods when they have a favor to ask, they throw spit-balls at his image!

The solemn cat of Japan, who never plays with her tail, because it is nothing but a stump, is as great a pet of the youngsters as ours. Instead of "Kitty" they call it "Chop-pi," and here is a little song to a cat, which I take from *St. Nicholas*, to show you what sort of songs your Japanese sister sings:

"Chop-pi! Chop-pi!
Come here! Come here!
If you'll only catch those naughty rats.
I'll give you a feast for the best of cats.
There now! you think
If the sea is bad,
Your favorite fish
Cannot be had;
But I'll bustle about
And find some trout.
Chop-pi! Chop-pi!
Don't you hear;
Gow! Gow!
Run my dear."

You must have, too, a Japanese lullaby, such as mothers sing to their dear little yellow, satiny babies.

"Sleep, my child, sleep my child,
Where is thy nurse gone?
She's gone to the mountains
To buy thee sweetmeats.
What shall she buy thee?
The thundering drum, the bamboo fife,
The trundling man, or the paper kite?"

A STREET IN JEDDO.

There are other pets in Japan besides cats; in fact, the little people are very fond of animals. Sometimes tiny bantam chicks are petted and played with, and even a tree-toad will not be despised. Almost any animal is welcome for a pet, and a little water-turtle with a fringed tail is the delight of their hearts.

These same little people are very fond of picnics, which they

COUNTRY RESTAURANT.

enjoy rather differently from our fashion. You see, they set up a screen, or a sort of curtain, around their particular spot of ground, and then they are almost as private as in one of their houses.

If they happen to run short of things to eat, they may provide themselves on the way from a country restaurant like this,

A PICNIC.

where everybody seems to be having a good time, and their famous mountain is seen in the distance.

But not all Japanese life is fun and frolic. Here is a very grave man indeed, the keeper of a curiosity shop, where we outside barbarians should go to buy vases and figures, and other fine and beautiful things to bring home with us, though perhaps

THE MOST SOLEMN OF ALL.

we should not leave our shoes outside, as you see most of his customers do.

And there's a still more serious person in Japan, the soldier. See him on page 403. Life seems to be a very sober matter indeed to this gentleman.

CURIOSITY SHOP.

The most solemn personage in all Japan is, of course, among the highest officers; and on page 400 you may see how very important they feel themselves, and how very humble must be the common men who appear before them.

It is New Year's day, and the visitors are calling to offer the compliments of the season. They bow to the floor to salute the great man, who is seated on his mat with a guard behind him.

For a story that has been told around the fire-box to thousands of quaint little people, squatting around on mats, I shall quote one from Mitford's "Tales of old Japan."

The Battle of the Ape and the Crab.

"If a man thinks only of his own profit, and tries to benefit himself at the expense of others, he will incur the hatred of heaven. Men should lay up in their hearts the story of the battle of the ape and the crab, and teach it as a profitable lesson to their children.

"Once upon a time there was a crab who lived in a marsh in a certain part of the country. It fell out one day that, the crab having picked up a rice-cake, an ape, who had got a nasty hard persimmon-seed, came up and begged the crab to make an exchange with him. The crab, who was a simple-minded creature, agreed to this proposal; and they each went their way, the ape chuckling to himself at the good bargain he had made.

"When the crab got home, he planted the persimmon-seed in his garden, and as time slipped by it sprouted, and by degrees grew to be a big tree.

"The crab watched the growth of his tree with great delight; but when the fruit ripened and he was going to pluck it, the ape

SOLDIER OF JAPAN.

came in and offered to gather it for him. The crab consenting, the ape climbed up into the tree, and began eating all the ripe fruit himself, while he only threw down the sour persimmons to the crab, inviting him at the same time to eat heartily.

"The crab, however, was not pleased at this arrangement, and thought that it was his turn to play a trick upon the ape; so he called out to him to come down head foremost.

"The ape did as he was bid; and as he crawled down head foremost, the ripe fruit all came tumbling out of his pockets, and the crab, having picked up the persimmons, ran off and hid himself in a hole.

"The ape, seeing this, lay in ambush, and, as soon as the crab crept out of his hiding-place, gave him a sound drubbing and went home. Just at this time a friendly egg, and a bee, who were the apprentices of a certain rice-mortar, happened to pass that way, and seeing the crab's piteous condition tied up his wounds, and having escorted him home began to lay plans to be revenged upon the cruel ape.

"Having agreed upon a scheme, they all went to the ape's house in his absence, and each one having undertaken to play a certain part, they waited in secret for their enemy to come home.

"The ape, little dreaming of the mischief that was brewing, returned home, and having a fancy to drink a cup of tea, began lighting the fire in the hearth, when all of a sudden the egg, which was hidden in the ashes, burst with the heat, and bespattered the frightened ape's face so that he fled, howling with pain, and crying:

"'Oh! what an unlucky beast I am!

"Maddened with the heat of the burst egg, he tried to go to

the back of the house, when the bee darted out of a cupboard, and, a piece of seaweed, who had joined the party, coming up at the same time, the ape was surrounded by enemies.

"In despair he seized the clothes-rack and fought valiantly for a while; but he was no match for so many, and was obliged to run away, with the others in hot pursuit after him.

"Just as he was making his escape by a back door, however, the piece of seaweed tripped him up, and the rice-mortar, closing with him from behind, made an end of him.

"So the crab, having punished his enemy, went home in triumph, and lived ever after on terms of brotherly love with the seaweed and the mortar. Was there ever such a fine piece of fun?"

I promised in the beginning to tell you strange things about the little people of Asia.

Haven't I done it?

THE END.